RUTH & ESTHER

The Old Testament books of Ruth and Esther are marked by gripping narratives which deftly display God's wise, sovereign and saving purposes. In his expositional commentaries of these two books, David Strain engagingly unfolds their narratives, explains their immediate historical and their ultimate redemptive historical significance, and applies the text carefully to the lives of his readers. In Dr Strain's flowing prose, both the text and the theological truths imbedded in the text are explained with pastoral thoughtfulness and a deft appreciation of their place within the biblical canon. These are commentaries that preachers will benefit from and all Christians find hugely instructive. I heartily commend them.

Ian Hamilton
Associate Minister
Smithton Culloden Church, Inverness, Scotland

David Strain's expositions of Ruth and Esther are both insightful and delightful. With careful attention to the text in its context and a firm grasp of redemptive history, Strain guides the reader through the lives of these two women of God. He demonstrates how their experiences have so much to teach us about our own Christian experience, and he keeps our eyes focused on the Lord Jesus Christ though it all. Here is solid exposition combined with pastoral wisdom. If you are looking for a faithful and engaging commentary on these Biblical books, then you have found it.

Rhett P. Dodson
Senior Pastor
Grace Presbyterian Church, Hudson, Ohio

Ruth and Esther are two of the most charming stories in the Bible. Yet these carefully crafted accounts of two faithful women point beyond human factors to the invisible hand of the good and sovereign God. David Strain's engaging exposition calls people in bitter circumstances to believe that, somehow, God is using all things to save His people and establish the kingdom of His Son.

Joel R. Beeke
President
Puritan Reformed Theological Seminary, Grand Rapids, Michigan

With characteristic expository skill and pastoral sensitivity, David Strain opens up two books which are often consigned to a bygone age and obscure culture, demonstrating beyond doubt their living relevance to every century and exposing the challenges they pose to God's people in every age. Above all, Strain shows how both books, seen in the light of the big Bible picture, are meant to draw us to a greater knowledge of a covenant keeping God as He works His own perfect plan into history, turning the chaotic into His own 'eucatastrophe' to accomplish His perfect gospel objective in Christ Jesus. This well written, compelling devotional companion will be of immense help to those who want to get beyond two mere narratives and understand their pivotal place in Bible history.

Iver Martin
Principal
Edinburgh Theological Seminary, Edinburgh, Scotland

David Strain ministers God's word with theological depth, biblical breadth, Christological focus, devotional warmth, and literary skill. With a deft hand he leads us from the distant world of ancient Israel to the world we inhabit today. These studies of Ruth and Esther will prove illuminating and edifying for individuals, study groups, and teachers/preachers.

Terry L. Johnson
Senior Minister
Independent Presbyterian Church, Savannah, Georgia

In this book we are treated to a master class in contemporary preaching. We have rigorous exegetical preparation which, although hidden deep within the foundations, has clearly been done. We have relevant application to the issues facing Church and society in the Twenty-first century but most of all we have an author whose heart, voice and pen has a magnetic north tuned to the heart of the gospel: the Cross. One of the positives in our current culture is a rediscovery of the value of story. David Strain unpacks the stories of two young girls whose lives and experiences illustrate the purpose of providence. If you ever wonder why you are where you are in life, *Ruth & Esther* will give you food for thought.

David C Meredith
Mission Director
Free Church of Scotland

This is no dry commentary. David Strain has blessed both pastor and congregant by writing this volume on Ruth and Esther. Here is a commentary that exudes pastoral wisdom and heart-directed application flowing from thorough biblical exegesis and theological precision. As these pages are read, the student of Scripture should expect to witness the Lord's work, not only in the lives of Ruth and Esther, but also in their own.

Jason Helopoulos
Senior Pastor
University Reformed Church, East Lansing, Michigan

David Strain has helped to fill a much needed gap in expository literature. Reliable and Reformed expositions of Ruth and Esther are hard to come by. Dr Strain's *Ruth & Esther* models careful exegesis, clear doctrinal thinking, and pointed practical application, all the while never failing to show how these two Old Testament books point to Christ. Whether you are teaching or preaching these books or simply want to know God's Word better, *Ruth & Esther* has earned a place on your shelf.

Guy Prentiss Waters
James M. Baird, Jr. Professor of New Testament
Reformed Theological Seminary

David Strain has provided for us a well-done, faithful, effective and insightful commentary which can be read by any believer devotionally yet will be of significant value for preachers in sermon development as well as an inspirational asset for the serious Bible student.

Harry L. Reeder
Pastor Teacher
Briarwood Presbyterian Church, Birmingham, Alabama

RUTH & ESTHER

There is a Redeemer &
Sudden Reversals

David Strain

CHRISTIAN
FOCUS

David Strain is Senior Minister of First Presbyterian Church, Jackson, Mississippi. He is Chairman of the Board of Christian Witness to Israel (North America), and Covenener of the Twin Lakes Fellowship.

Copyright © 2018 David Strain

ISBN 978-1-5271-0234-7

10 9 8 7 6 5 4 3 2 1

Printed in 2018
by
Christian Focus Publications Ltd.,
Geanies House, Fearn, Ross-shire,
IV20 1TW, Scotland, U.K.

www.christianfocus.com

Cover design by Daniel van Straaten

Printed and bound by
Bell & Bain, Glasgow

Contents

*For Sheena, whom the Lord gave me
'for such a time as this'.*

Acknowledgements

This book has been a long time coming. I must thank William Mackenzie and Malcolm Maclean of Christian Focus Publications for their friendship, demonstrated especially clearly in their patience with me as I slowly pulled this material together. To the elders and members of the First Presbyterian Church of Jackson, Mississippi, I also owe a great debt. They endured the material in this volume in two series of Sunday evening expositions, and their love and enthusiasm for it has been an enormous encouragement to persevere in the task. This volume is dedicated to them, among whom it has been my life's greatest privilege to serve. May the Lord continue to bless you all.

David Strain
2018

Introduction to Ruth and Esther

There is something deep inside us all that is hard wired to respond to a good story. The books of Ruth and Esther stand out among the great stories of human history for their pathos, high drama, honest humanity, good humor, and spiritual depths. Unique in biblical literature, these two accounts focus on the lives of two women – a fact that immediately propels them to a place of special relevance in our cultural moment.

Ruth is a Moabite who married into a Jewish family. Hers is an outsider's tale; a story of desperation and marginalization, of hope almost lost and wonderfully regained. As we watch her find a home among the people of God in Bethlehem we learn to trace the threads of divine providence that bring her, not only into the heart of the covenant community, but into the heart of God's plan for the salvation of the nations. Ruth's story teaches us that God loves to save Moabites, and if there is room in His kingdom for Ruth, surely there is room for us. But it also teaches us something bigger. Not only does God delight to save outsiders and makes them insiders, He also loves to make use of unlikely instruments to accomplish His grand designs. From the union of Ruth and Boaz will descend David the King, and from David will descend Christ the King of Kings.

Esther's tale, on the other hand, begins after the exile some six hundred years later. She is a beautiful young Hebrew girl living in Susa, the capital of Ahasueras, the debauched ruler of the vast Persian Empire. While Ruth's story focuses on the rather mundane dynamics of a peasant family during the time of the Judges, Esther's story plays out in the palace precincts of a despotic king, as she maneuvers her way through the potentially lethal intrigues of life in the imperial court. As horrific accounts of the manipulation and exploitation of women by powerful men continue to make headlines today, Esther's story rings true. The exiting pace with which the narrative develops and the laugh-out-loud ironies with which it concludes must not be allowed to obscure the dark tragedy with which it begins. It is the account of a young girl snatched from her home to live in a king's harem (with all that that implies). Here, surely, is a word for our day.

Famously, the name of God is never once mentioned in the book. But this absence, rather than obscure the spiritual significance of the story, only serves to highlight what is really going on. The absence is glaring, forcing us to conclude for ourselves what the narrator never explicitly states. And this is one of the book's most pastorally helpful contributions. While God is never mentioned we cannot avoid seeing His handiwork in every twist and turn of the narrative. And in this way the narrator trains us to trust the providence of God, even when the apparent absence of God seems to us so glaring. Despite the surface differences of time and place, culture and class, in the end Esther's story, like Ruth's, celebrates the providence of our Sovereign God, who works by improbable means to save His people (1 Cor. 1:18-31). Esther becomes the savior of her people and the destroyer of her enemies. And in this she is a type of Christ, who, though brutalized by wicked men, is made both savior and judge of all.

Ruth

Authorship and Date

We cannot assert with any certainty the identity of the author of the book of Ruth. However, the emphasis throughout on the theme of kingship, beginning in 1:2 with Elimelech (whose name means *My God is King)* and climaxing in 4:18-22 with the genealogy of King David, likely locates its composition sometime during the rise or reign of David, about 1000 B.C. The Talmud says that Ruth was written by the prophet Samuel,[1] and while this is widely disputed by scholars who point out that Samuel was dead before David rose to the throne, there are reasons why this suggestion remains at least plausible. Samuel knew God's purpose for the Davidic kingship, having anointed David privately as the future king long before his formal ascension to the throne. The exclusion of Solomon's name from the genealogy at the end of Ruth suggests that the book provides an apologetic for David's reign, which only makes sense if the book was written during his lifetime. In the end, the anonymity of the book ought to be respected and no more ink need be spilt on speculating about its author.

Purpose and Themes

The time of composition matters because it helps us understand its purpose. Ruth is not simply a love story, or a tale of a widow's redemption. It is an apologetic for David's kingship. We ought not to conclude from this that Ruth is

---

1. For a helpful discussion of this Talmudic tradition and the range of scholarly opinion concerning it, see John J. Yeo, *Ruth,* in *A Biblical Theological Introduction to the Old Testament: The Gospel Promised,* Miles V. Van Pelt, ed. (Wheaton, IL: Crossway, 2016), pp. 400-01.

not history, merely a piece of Davidic propaganda. After all, if that is all that it was, why highlight his Moabite ancestry or the wrong-headed abandonment of the Promised Land that led to the destitution of Naomi's family? But none of these facts are omitted. Here is David's unvarnished family history. Of course, it is precisely in these potentially embarrassing themes, that we learn what kind of king David was called to be, and beyond him, what kind of king great David's greater son would be. He would be a king who would bring rest to His people, just as Boaz brought rest to Naomi and Ruth. He will be a king under whose reign outsiders might find refuge beneath the wings of the Almighty.

The setting of the book is also important. Ruth occurs during the time of the Judges (1:1), when the people of Israel were wracked by repeated cycles of spiritual decline, divine chastisement, and spiritual renewal. The refrain that there was no king in Israel punctuates the book of Judges (17:6; 18:1; 19:1; 21:25). The book of Ruth tells us that God was at work to provide for His people, not only on a national scale by raising up judges to save them, but also on an unnoticed level, in the quiet return of these two destitute women from an overly prolonged sojourn in Moab. While the TV news headlines in Israel each evening would feature the exploits of judges or the damage of invading enemies, the arrival of Naomi and Ruth only caused a stir for a day or two in Bethlehem. And yet it would be here, rather than in Ehud's black-ops mission or Samson's great feats of strength that God's ultimate provision for the salvation of His people would be found.

Esther

Authorship and Date

Likely composed around 400 B.C., after the reign of Ahasueras came to an end, the authorship of Esther is unknown. Some have argued that the original author was Persian, thus accounting for the apparent absence of God in the narrative. However, the story is a vindication of the Jewish people in the face of a terrible anti-Semitism, providing an apologetic for the feast of Purim, which commemorates the great deliverance the Hebrews experienced as a result of Esther's courage. We conclude that the author(s) of Esther were Jewish exiles, likely living in the Persian empire. They wrote to equip God's people to live as strangers in a strange land, reminding them of the hope that they may yet have in the sovereign Lord who defends His people.

Purpose and Themes

Jeremiah 29:4-7 offered what Barry Webb has called 'an appropriate lifestyle for Jews in exile, the basic principle being a recognition of the interdependence of the Jewish community and its host environment.'[1] The book of Esther makes plain however that the implementation of that policy is far from easy. That the names of the Jewish protagonists (Esther and Mordecai) are probably theonyms, referencing Ishtar and Marduk respectively, so suggesting a significant level of cultural assimilation. The lack of mention of the God of Israel, especially in the dialogue between Esther and her

---

1. Barry Webb, *Five Festal Garments: Christian Reflections on the Song of Songs, Ruth, Lamentations, Ecclesiastes, Esther* (Downers Grove, IL: Apollos, IVP, 2000), p. 118.

uncle, further reinforces this impression. It is one thing for Haman or Ahasueras to sound like unbelievers. They were. But what are we to make of the absence of God even in the private speech of our two heroes?

Far from generating perplexity however, it is here that the book makes an important pastoral contribution. The narrative unfolds in a world where Esther is not in control of her own destiny and in this she is the embodiment of the fate of her people. Esther, like the exiled Jews living in Susa, is completely at the mercy of her Persian overlords. The action unfolds around a series of banquets. Life and death is meted out, the lusts of a tyrant are sated, high political office stripped away in an instant and just as quickly bestowed upon another, amidst the whimsy and indulgence of Ahasueras' latest party. There is no idealization, no sugar coating, no polishing away the rough edges when it comes to the account we are given of power and its abuse. At a time when the weak and vulnerable are victimized on an industrial scale, when the lives of women and children are trafficked around the world, when the strong leverage their power in order to gratify their lusts, Esther speaks a word we badly need to hear. For it is against this dark backdrop that the story unfolds of a sudden reversal (9:1-22), not just for Esther, who rises to become queen, but for the Jews who end the account victorious over their enemies. While the feasts of Ahasueras were fraught with moral and political danger, the narrative concludes with a new feast, a feast of the Jews, the feast of Purim, celebrating unexpected victory snatched from the jaws of inevitable defeat.

But this theme of victory in the book is, of course, only the latest round in the cosmic conflict between the kingdom of God and the kingdom of Satan that frames the storyline of the whole Bible. In Esther this conflict focuses on Haman 'the enemy of the Jews' (3:10; 9:24) and Mordecai. Haman is an Agagite, while Mordecai is a descendant of Kish. That the sons of Agag and Kish the Benjamite should be enemies would not have come as a surprise to Jewish readers who remember the clash between Israel's king Saul and Agag in 1 Samuel 15. Saul failed to fulfill God's will in destroying Agag. Mordecai, Saul's descendant, does not. But this ancient rivalry is expressive of the fundamental clash between the Seed of the woman and the seed of the serpent in Genesis 3:15, a clash that does not climax till the Cross. There we see the ultimate great reversal: life out of death, victory from apparent defeat.

And it is in this way that the absence of explicit mentions of God becomes a device to make His presence and activity glaringly obvious. The theme of an overarching providence, superintending the caprice of Ahasueras and thwarting the malice of Haman, cannot be avoided. Without once speaking of God, the book of Esther demands that we never lose sight of Him, who works whether we acknowledge Him or not, to keep His ancient promises.

Ruth
There is a Redeemer

I

Subtle Steps
(Ruth 1:1-5)

When I pastored a small church in central London, England, I would occasionally take the Underground, the Tube, to get to our evening worship services, and then get a lift home afterwards with one of our ruling elders who lived near our home in the northeast of the city. He was a wonderful brother, a veterinarian who had emigrated from Tasmania and settled with his wife in London. He seemed to know the back roads and alternate routes of the inner city like the back of his hand. With some regularity, since we were in a busy city, we'd find our path blocked by road works or some other obstruction as we tried to make it home after the service. And he would immediately take evasive action turning left and right, in what seemed to me a bewildering series of white-knuckle maneuvers. On at least one occasion I remember him mounting the sidewalk and creating a path where one did not exist before. Left and right we'd turn until I was totally lost. But then somehow, suddenly, almost inexplicably, we would emerge onto familiar streets and a clear path home.

The book of Ruth is about one Ephrathite family from Bethlehem in Judah that takes some wrong turns as they seek to navigate the complexities of life. They take a detour, and it has disastrous consequences. But, as I hope we'll see, it is, in fact, the Lord God Himself who sits at the wheel, governing and superintending the details of their lives. Although the route may at first seem improbable, and the many twists and turns in the road bewildering, He brings them safely through in the end nonetheless.

If you've read the Book of Ruth, you will know that it is a delightful short story full of pathos and beauty. It's a wonderful romance, and who doesn't enjoy a good love story? It's a story about an outsider, a Moabite girl, a girl with a past, who finds a place among the people of God. Outsiders can find a home among God's children because of God's grace. That's part of the message of the book of Ruth. But far more even than that, the story of Ruth is a story of God's sovereign governance of all things; a record of the stunning skill with which our Lord weaves the details, and, yes, even the tragedies, of our lives together for our salvation. In fact, Ruth's great value lies in helping us take in just how grand and expansive the scope of God's sovereign love and care for His people really is.

It's a story, which at first, though undoubtedly beautiful, moving even, might appear insignificant in the grand scheme of things. It is a narrative about an unremarkable Moabite girl and the no-name Ephrathite family into which she married. So, while there's drama, and no small degree of fascination, to be found in the way the story is told, the book of Ruth may, nevertheless, leave us scratching our heads. We wonder if the personal details of one insignificant family's struggle to survive amid hard times are really worth inclusion, alongside the creation account, say, or the story of the parting of the Red Sea, in the canon of Holy Scripture. After all, there's nothing supernatural in the book of Ruth. There is nothing even spectacular or unusual in the book of Ruth. It's all so terribly... normal.

And that is precisely the point. The promises of God pertain not just to the spectacular or the epoch-shaping events of history; they are promises for the mundane and the ordinary and the normal. Ruth tells us that the God who spoke the world into being, who parted the Red Sea, who thundered on Sinai and who raised Jesus from the tomb, is the same God who is intimately involved in the fateful decision a father made to move his family to Moab. He is the same God who superintends the cascade of tragedy that follows that decision, and He is the one who leads the tattered and broken remnants of Elimelech's household back to Bethlehem to make a new start. The book of Ruth is designed to teach us that there is no point in our lives where God is not present and working all things together for the good of those who love Him: not in the desperation of economic catastrophe, not in the darkness of bereavement, not in the loneliness of personal isolation. There is no place in your life that God's sovereign hand of goodness and grace is not at work, mysteriously, sometimes in unseen ways, to govern and direct all things for your everlasting good, if by grace you are a child of His. Though you may not be able to see it, the book of Ruth teaches us to trust that it is so nonetheless.

And so as we turn our attention now to the opening verses of Ruth chapter 1, and to a domestic scene that may mirror scenes that have played out in our own families, we need to be careful not to write them off as insignificant. Actually, the details of the life of Elimelech's family, as we meet them in verses 1-5, are pregnant with divine purpose. In particular, we can see two things here.

1. Sin Often Ensnares by Subtle Steps

The story begins in verse 1 with an ominous statement. The action all takes place 'in the days when the Judges ruled'. The period covered in the book of Judges runs from 1200–1020 b.c. And the story of Ruth seems to take place relatively early within that time frame, a point suggested by the fact that the central figure of Boaz is called 'the son of Rahab, the prostitute.'

Rahab lived in Jericho in the period before the Judges, during Israel's conquest of Canaan under the leadership of Joshua. But regardless of when precisely we locate the action, anyone who reads through the history of Israel recorded in the book of Judges will know that it was a time of general chaos in the spiritual life of the people of God. It was marked by dramatic pendulum swings from covenant obedience to reckless idolatry and forbidden alliances with pagan nations. It was a period of profound moral and spiritual instability, in which Israel spiraled downwards towards apostasy, so that, as the last verse of the book of Judges puts it, 'Everyone did what was right in his own eyes.' And it is into the maelstrom of this period in the life of God's people, this one little Ephrathite family is cast, like so much flotsam, blown and tossed by the prevailing spiritual and cultural winds.

It is also important to see that this was a time, not just of spiritual crisis, but of economic crisis as well. 'There was a famine in the land.' As one scholar explains, 'The highly variable rainfall in the highlands of ancient Canaan were always a factor that the village farmers and herdsmen had to contend with year after year.'[1] In other words, for an agrarian society like this one, a few successive seasons without rain could precipitate a national catastrophe of unimaginable proportions: crops failed, cattle died, people starved.

Onto this grim stage steps 'a man of Bethlehem in Judah'. There is an irony here that Hebrew readers of the book of Ruth would immediately have recognized, designed by the writer to highlight the chaotic, upside down nature of life in the days of the Judges. Things are not the way they're supposed to be. It's all back to front. And the irony of Elimelech's hometown makes that plain. The name *Bethlehem* means 'House of Bread'. Elimelech and his family came from the breadbasket of Israel, and when there is a famine in the house of bread, things are grim indeed.

But just about fifty miles away, across the Dead Sea, on the high plateau of Moab, there was no famine, and so Elimelech makes what must have seemed like a necessary and wise decision. He took his wife and his two sons, and he went 'to sojourn in the land of Moab'. Now that word 'sojourn' is important. It tells us that Elimelech had no intention of settling in Moab. It was a temporary visit. They were economic refugees, driven by necessity, fleeing famine for survival's sake. So who could blame Elimelech for this decision? Surely, he was acting in the best economic and material interests of his wife and children. That's what husbands are meant to do. And the text tells us he planned all along to return to Bethlehem as soon as he could; they were merely *sojourners*.

But, however well-intentioned, it would prove a fateful decision. Mahlon and Chilion, Elimelech and Naomi's two

---

1. Victor H. Matthews, *Judges and Ruth* (New York: Cambridge University Press, 2004), p.218.

boys, married Moabite girls and they quickly put down roots. Elimelech, for his part, never made it back to Bethlehem. He died in Moab. And as verse 4 tells us, ten whole years were to pass, until eventually Mahlon and Chilion would join their father in a Moabite graveyard. They left Naomi, and her two pagan daughters-in-law, Orpah and Ruth, destitute and vulnerable at a time when, to be an unmarried woman, and particularly a widow, was to live without means of support or security. What seemed like a wise plan at its inception was a catastrophe at its end. It *looked* like a shortcut, but it was quite literally a 'dead end.' The story of Elimelech's family, as I'm sure you are already beginning to see, is a tragedy. But it's more than that. It is a warning. Notice the subtle steps by which sin ensnared this man and his household:

(i) Step One: A Failure of Wisdom

Elimelech has assessed his circumstances and decided his course of action based on the economic crisis in his own country and the economic opportunity in the neighboring country. He attempted to read providence, but seems to have done so autonomously and independently. He was trying to make sense of what was happening based entirely on the data available to him in the things he could see and touch and weigh and count. But Elimelech ought to have known better. When the author of the book of Ruth tells us in the very first verse that the action takes place in the days when the Judges ruled, and that there was a famine in the land, he is doing much more than simply painting a picture of spiritual chaos or economic crisis. He is making a profound theological statement.

For Israel, a famine in the land was more than a failure of proper planning or wise land and water management. It was about more than the appropriate stewardship of natural resources. At this point in salvation history, a famine in the land was one of the covenant curses promised by God for Israel's failure to be faithful to Him. In Deuteronomy, Moses had told the people:

> If you will not obey the voice of the Lord your God or be careful to do all his commandments and his statutes that I command you

today, then all these curses shall come upon you and overtake you. Cursed shall you be in the city, and cursed shall you be in the field. Cursed shall be your basket and your kneading bowl. Cursed shall be the fruit of your womb and the fruit of your ground, the increase of your herds and the young of your flock… You shall carry much seed into the field and shall gather in little, for the locust shall consume it. You shall plant vineyards and dress them, but you shall neither drink of the wine nor gather the grapes, for the worm shall eat them. You shall have olive trees throughout all your territory, but you shall not anoint yourself with the oil… (Deut. 28:15-18, 38-40).

In other words, when Elimelech looked at the famine, he *ought* to have read it through the lens of the warnings of Holy Scripture. He ought to have connected the moral crisis of rebellion against God in the spiritual life of Israel with the famine sweeping through the land of Israel. He ought to have read providence *in light of the Word of God*, and heard, in the sharp pangs of physical hunger, the alarms and warnings of the God of covenant faithfulness, who was working to reclaim His people from rebellion and backsliding and sin. Elimelech ought *not* to have fled the land. He ought instead to have returned to God.

When we try to understand God's providence in general, and the hard providence of our sufferings in particular, without the interpretive lenses of Holy Scripture firmly in place, we will always tend to misunderstand them and misinterpret them. But when we interpret providence through Scripture, we will learn to hear in our sufferings, in our pains and our trials, what Elimelech ought not to have missed. They are, as C. S. Lewis once put it, 'God's megaphone,' designed to awaken us to our need for Him. 'God whispers to us in our pleasures,' said Lewis, 'speaks in our conscience, but shouts in our pains: it is his megaphone to rouse a deaf world.'[2] Or as the book of Hebrews makes the same point: 'We are to endure hardship as discipline, for God is treating you as sons…. For the moment, all discipline seems painful rather than pleasant, but later it yields the peaceful fruit of righteousness to those

---

2. C. S. Lewis, *The Problem of Pain*, Harper Collins, (New York, NY: HarperOne, 2001), pp. 90-91.

who have been trained by it' (Heb. 12:7, 11). God was calling
to Israel in their sufferings – disciplining them – and Elimelech
would have known that, had he read their trials through the
lens of scripture. Instead of fleeing from the land, he ought
to have fled to God for mercy.

But that's not what happened. Elimelech took his family
from the one place in the world God had ordained to bless
and put His presence – the land of Israel – and he brought
them down into pagan Moab, to the home of the ancestral
enemies of the Lord and His people. Oh, it was only supposed
to be for a little while – only until the crisis had passed. They
would only be *sojourners* in Moab. But how many times have
we rationalized our drifting away from God's priorities in
pursuit of our personal agendas, just like that? I'll take that
job. It's only for a few years, after all. Surely we can tough it
out without a decent church for that long? Who cares about
the fourth or fifth or sixth glass of wine on Saturday night? So
long as I make it to church on Sunday morning, it's all good,
right? I'll indulge today and rededicate myself tomorrow.
I'll go away to a 'far country' because it seems right in my
own eyes now, but it's just for a little while. But ten long,
painful years went by, and they were still there, ensnared
by a cascade of fateful and foolish decisions. Let's beware
the subtle steps by which sin ensnares us. Elimelech's good
intentions were no protection against sin's sly tactics. You
might mean well. It may look wise. But if you try to read
God's providence in your life without submitting to God's
precepts in His Word, you will always, always go astray. You
will justify your disobedience by claiming, 'necessity drove
me to it,' but your good intentions will not inoculate you
against sin's ensnaring power. There was a terrible failure of
wisdom here.

(ii) Step Two: A Failure of Piety

Notice the names in our passage carefully. We're not simply
being given the *dramatis personae* (the list of characters). These
names are significant. Naomi means 'pleasant', but Mahlon
means 'sickly' and Chilion means 'frail'. At this point we are
probably asking, 'What were their parents *thinking*, naming
their boys Sickly and Frail? The poor boys must have had a

terribly hard time on the playground at school.' But in all probability, their names reflected the terrible effects of the famine during the circumstances of their birth. They *were* sickly and frail. That's how hard things must have been.

But the central character in these verses is, of course, Elimelech himself, and his name means 'My God is king'. And that's an encouraging name, to be sure, particularly at a time when, as Judges 21:25 puts it, 'There was no king in Israel. Everyone did what was right in his own eyes.' Here is Elimelech, it seems, born to a family concerned to raise him so that, no matter the prevailing cultural winds, he would know and confess that 'My God is king'. Here is a man who was raised in a context that acknowledged the Lordship of Almighty God in his life. God the Lord was Israel's King. His name signals a fundamental commitment and submission to the rule of God.

But when you examine the book of Ruth scene by scene, you will notice something that directly conflicts with the spiritual encouragement Elimelech's name seems to give us. Every other scene in the storyline of the book of Ruth, mentions God explicitly (in each case, interestingly, in the context of direct speech). He is invoked, called upon, prayed to in every single scene – in every scene except this one. Here the name of God is completely absent, except as it appears in abbreviated form in Elimelech's name itself. It is a striking irony that the man named for submission to the rule and Lordship of Almighty God does not acknowledge Him and does not seek His face. He doesn't call on His name. He is the *only* major character in the *only* scene in the *entire* book of Ruth that fails to do so.

Do you see the subtle strategy that sin has used in the life of this little family to leave them broken and shattered, bereft and destitute? Elimelech, the man whose name leads us to expect godliness, turns his back on God's people and God's place. He misreads providence, neglects scripture warnings, and he does not seek God's face. And soon his children intermarry with pagan girls in violation of God's law. A temporary sojourn turns into a long-term stay, punctuated by the deaths of each of the three men who could lead the home and ensure its welfare and future. What a terrifying enemy sin can be: subtle, conniving, oblique, persuasive, appearing wise, always plausible, and always, always deadly in the end if we listen to its lies. Sin often ensnares by subtle steps. But the story does not end there.

2. God Often Leads by Hard Providences

The downward spiral for Elimelech's family reaches rock bottom at last in verse 5, as the three widows, Naomi, Orpah, and Ruth are left destitute and alone in Moab. It is a heart-rending scene of utter misery and loss. But it's clear that this catastrophe provides the set up for the rest of the story.

There is a divine purpose above and beyond the mis-guided plan Elimelech hatched in Bethlehem. God has been at work in sending the family to Moab, governing even their sin, for His holy ends, incorporating Ruth and Orpah into this Hebrew household, all of it carefully setting the stage for the drama to follow.

Without Elimelech's fateful decision to flee the famine, without Mahlon and Chilion taking Moabite wives, without the death of all three of the men in the home, Ruth would never have become the ancestor of Jesus Christ. The family line of Messiah would never have been established. There would be no gospel, no salvation for the nations, no remedy for sin, no answer to those who have been subtly ensnared by sin themselves, if Elimelech hadn't taken a wrong turn and gone to Moab, and Ruth hadn't married into the family.

Isn't it easy to repeat Romans 8:28? It comes to our lips so readily: 'And we know that for those who love God all things work together for good, for those who are called according to his purpose.' We write it in get-well-soon cards and repeat it to one another in times of stress. And so we should. What a precious text it is. But just how far has its truth penetrated your heart? Does God work all things together? *All* things? Elimelech's sin? The tragic deaths of the head of the household and his two sons? The destitution of Naomi and her pagan daughters-in-law? Does God work the darkest, sorest, ugliest, most shameful, most painful trials together for good? That is the hard and hopeful message of Romans 8:28 and Ruth 1:1-5. It's not a greeting card platitude. It is a gritty declaration of fact for real-world trials. However low into the shadows of loss you may sink or have your heart pierced through with sorrow and inexplicable suffering, even this God works for good – even this – in ways beyond our comprehension, leading ultimately, even if not immediately, to our eternal welfare.

The tragedy in Elimelech's home ensured that Messiah would be born of Ruth's line to be Himself submerged one day into the darkest pit of loss and sorrow and pain. Though sin often ensnares by subtle steps, praise God that He often works by hard providences. And the great proof and demonstration of that is the cross of His Son, the hardest providence of them all, by which our salvation has been secured.

2

The Journey Home
(Ruth 1:6-22)

I have always enjoyed Christian biography. It helps take the rich truths of the Bible and makes them concrete, showing us the strengths and weaknesses, the sins and successes of real people not so very different from ourselves, whom God nevertheless used mightily. Reading their lives helps us to read our own more honestly. As we turn to Ruth 1:6-22, the second scene in the book, there is something of that same phenomenon taking place. We are helped to see the ways of God with us, as we trace them in the lives of the three women caught up in this whirlwind of suffering and loss.

We pick up the story in verse 6 as Naomi and her daughters-in-law, Ruth and Orpah, are left destitute and mourning. But word has reached them in the fields of Moab that 'the LORD had visited his people' back home in Judah and provided food for them. The famine in the land was an expression of divine discipline. And, as such, it was designed to awaken His people and call them back to Himself, which is why God's discipline is only ever temporary in the lives of His children. It is never arbitrary or endless. It has an end and a result in view. And so now He has visited them in mercy and provided once again their daily bread. Moab was supposed to be the place of plenty for this little family. Instead, it became a scene of utter devastation. But now that God has visited Israel, Naomi resolves to make the journey home.

In fact, that word 'return' is crucial in understanding the rest of the chapter. It appears in almost every verse in one form or another. Verse 6: 'Then she arose with her daughters in law to return...' Verse 7: 'they went on the way to return to the land of Judah.' Verse 8: 'Naomi said to her daughters in law, "Go, return..."' Verse 10: 'No, we will return with you...' Verse 11: 'Naomi said, "turn back."' Verse 12: 'Turn back.' Verse 15: 'Your sister-in-law has gone back... return after your sister in law.' Verse 16: 'Do not urge me to leave you or to return.' Verse 22: 'So Naomi returned, and Ruth the Moabite, her daughter-in-law with her, who returned from the country of Moab.' This is a chapter about returning.

But the return journeys of each of these three women are very different indeed. And as we examine each of them, like any good biographical sketch, I hope that reading their lives will help us read our own more honestly in the sight of Almighty God. In fact, the stories of Orpah, Ruth, and Naomi each epitomize three very different, but very common, responses to the Lord, especially in His sovereign, providential dealings with us, particularly when suffering and hardships strike. In Orpah, we might say we have a picture of the almost-believer. Then in Ruth, we have a picture of a new believer. And then finally in Naomi, we have a picture of a backslidden believer.

1. Orpah: The Almost Believer

In verses 6 and 7, the three women set off together for the land of Judah, but Naomi knew that she could offer her daughters-in-law no prospects of improvement in their destitute circumstances should they continue with her. And so she urged them in verse 8, 'Go, return, each of you to her mother's house. May the Lord deal kindly with you, as you have dealt with the dead and with me. The Lord grant that you may find rest, each of you in the house of her husband.'

Naomi blessed her daughters-in-law, by invoking the covenant name of Almighty God, and sought to send them back home to their Moabite families. She knew that their best hopes of a better life lay in finding new husbands, and she knew it would be extremely unlikely that any Israelite would even notice a widowed Moabite girl. Just how grave the situation was will become clear later in the story, when Naomi sees that she cannot dissuade Ruth from coming with her all the way home. She doesn't thank her daughter-in-law for sticking with her. There are no hugs and kisses. All we are told is that 'she said no more' (v. 18). Silence is the best she could manage, because Naomi knew just how hard it was going to be for a Moabitess in the land of Judah.

And as the story will later make plain, Naomi's concerns are not without merit. When they do finally arrive at Bethlehem, and the whole town is stirred up, in verse 19 the women ask only, 'Is this Naomi?' They seem to ignore poor Ruth altogether. There's not a word about the Moabite girl tagging along. One commentator even suggests that there 'seems to have been an unspoken communal conspiracy not to mention the Moabitess'.[1]

It was this kind of reception Naomi seeks to spare her daughters-in-law at the beginning of their return journey. She knew very well that, in those days, to be a Moabite (not to mention a widow) in Judah was to be marked as an outcast. And so, in verses 8 and 9, she was trying hard to spare her two daughters-in-law the grief that their circumstances would, so far as she knew, inevitably entail.

But the initial reaction to Naomi's first speech on the part of these two Moabite girls tells us that, at the least, these three women have become very dear to one another. She kissed them, and they all wept together, and both Ruth and Orpah said, 'No, we will return with you to your people' (v. 10). And so Naomi doubled down on her insistence that the girls not follow her: 'Turn back, my daughters, why will you go with me? Have I yet sons in my womb that they may become your husbands?' (vv. 11-12).

That seems to us a very strange thing to say, but Naomi is talking about the law, established in Deuteronomy 25, that provided for what's called levirate marriage. A levirate marriage required a brother-in-law to replace a deceased husband in order to provide heirs, thus continuing the family name and preserving the family's inheritance in the Land of Promise. And though it seems strange to us, it was nevertheless a matter of enormous cultural importance in

---

1. Iain M. Duguid, *Esther and Ruth* (Phillipsburg, NJ: P & R Publishing, 2005), p. 144.

those days. But Naomi was telling her daughters-in-law that there was simply no possibility of that for them should they come with her. The situation was hopeless.

But now look carefully at verse 14: 'Then they lifted up their voices and wept again. And Orpah kissed her mother-in-law, but Ruth clung to her.' Orpah, as verse 15 confirms, took Naomi's advice and went back to Moab. She *started* to follow. She *began* the journey. It looked for a while like Naomi would have two daughters-in-law attach themselves to the people of God in the land of God. But Naomi's bleak portrait of a hopeless future apparently overcame any sense of personal loyalty to her mother-in-law that Orpah felt. And so she turned back. Both Ruth and Orpah walked along the same road together for a while, both responded in the same way to the same circumstances for a season, but while Ruth went on, Orpah turned back.

Some who read this will have made their own journey from Moab to Bethlehem. You have heard how the Lord has visited His people, and you have turned your backs on the world and come to Jesus Christ. But there have been those who have walked beside you on the road for a season. They seemed to offer bright hope that, like you, they had come to trust in the God of covenant mercy who had visited His people. But when the prospects ahead began to look bleak, and the real cost of making the journey became apparent, then they soon turned back. 'There are very many in the world,' wrote the Puritan Matthew Mead, 'that are almost, and yet but almost Christians; many that are near heaven, and yet are never the nearer; many that are within a little of salvation, and yet shall never enjoy the least salvation; they are within sight of heaven, and yet shall never have a sight of God.'[2]

Maybe you attend church and are often to be seen around Christians because of your wife or husband, your parent or a friend. They follow Jesus, and you are deeply committed to them. You honor them, much as Orpah honored Naomi. But personal loyalty, the religion of your parents, the tradition of your family, is never enough to break the pull of Moab.

2. Rev. Matthew Mead, *The Almost Christian Discovered: Or, the False Professor Tried and Cast* (CreateSpace Independent Publishing Platform, 2013), p. 28.

The world always looks like an easier home than the difficult prospects that face anyone who seeks a place among God's people. If all you have is love for tradition or love for family, but you have no love for the Lord Jesus Christ Himself, inevitably you will turn back. Your heart will be like the seed sown in rocky soil in Matthew 13:5. It immediately sprang up, but since it has no depth of soil, the sun scorched it. And since there was no root, it withered away. You are the one, Jesus says, who 'hears the word and immediately receives it with joy, yet has no root in himself, but endures for a while, and when tribulation or persecution arises on account of the word, immediately he falls away.' Oh, how we need to search our hearts in light of Orpah's turning back. Do not be like the rich young man in Matthew 19:22, who, after speaking with Jesus, went away sorrowful, for 'he had great possessions'. The cost of following Jesus was too great for him to bear. The lure of Moab is strong. Be sure that your pilgrimage to the Land of Promise is not a temporary diversion from the broad road that leads to destruction. Do not be an almost believer.

2. Ruth: The New Believer

Orpah turned back. And in verse 15 Naomi urged Ruth to do the same: 'See your sister-in-law has gone back to her people and to her gods; return after your sister-in-law.' But Ruth replied, in words that are justly among the most famous in the Old Testament: 'Do not urge me to leave you or to return from following you. For where you go I will go, and where you lodge, I will lodge. Your people shall be my people, and your God my God. Where you die, I will die, and there I will be buried. May the Lord do so to me, and more also, if anything but death parts me from you.' What has happened to Ruth to produce this extraordinary declaration of commitment, when Orpah had already buckled under the pressure and turned back? There is only one explanation: Ruth has been converted.[3]

---

3. It is, of course, possible that Ruth came to trust in YHWH at an earlier point. I argue that, in the context of the narrative, it is best to view Ruth's speech to Naomi as evidence of a more recent conversion. Her coming to faith, in my view, is one fruit of the hard providence of God in the life of this family and is best understood coming at this crucial turning point, as the family decides either to stay together, or break apart and return to the land and to the Lord.

Now, Naomi, of course, can hardly be said to be the best model of evangelism. Her approach is almost brutal. If her daughters-in-law follow her to Israel, she insists that things will only go from bad to worse. And in verse 15 she even seems determined to send Ruth back to her paganism, just like Orpah. 'Go back to your gods,' she says. Clearly, not all is well in the heart of Naomi, as we'll see in the next section. But the Lord can draw a straight line with a crooked stick, and here He used an embittered Naomi to bring heartbroken Ruth to Himself.

Ruth's conversion comes out in a variety of ways in the text. First, notice for example, that Ruth echoes the language of God's covenant promise to Israel. He told them, in Exodus 6:7, 'I will take you to be my people, and I will be your God.' But now Ruth turns God's promise around, and declares, 'Your people shall be my people, and your God shall be my God.' She takes God's covenant for her own and identifies herself with those whom God has redeemed. Ruth has faced all the discouragements that Naomi has thrown in her path. She knows that, humanly speaking, she has very few prospects for a brighter future in Judah. She watched her sister-in-law, whom she clearly loves, leave for greener pastures in Moab. She has lost everything, with no earthly hope of recovery if she continues to travel the road from Moab to Bethlehem.

The only explanation that can account for her determination to make the journey at all is that her heart has changed profoundly. She has been saved by grace through faith in the God of Israel, whose covenant name she invoked directly in verse 17: 'May the LORD (Yahweh) do so to me, and more also, if anything but death parts me from you.' It is the name by which God had revealed Himself to Israel as their deliverer and savior, the name that signaled His covenant love and faithfulness to them in remembering His promises and bringing them up out of Egypt. 'This God, I take as my God. His people, I take as my people. I cannot leave you, Naomi, because I cannot leave the God I love. I cling to you Naomi because I cling to him.'

Here's the great difference between the almost-believer and a genuine convert to Jesus Christ. The almost-believer follows on the path because of personal loyalties, because of the love of a mother-in-law who has lost everything. But in the end, however strong those loyalties may be, the almost-believer turns back. When the hardships of life press in, the almost-believer finds the familiar comforts of Moab easier than the cost of life among the people of God. But the new believer counts the cost. There is no sugar coating it. The new believer knows that to follow Jesus means to take up the cross. The new believer knows, as Ruth knew, that 'through many tribulations we must enter the kingdom of God' (Acts 14:22). But God Himself has come to capture her heart nonetheless, and so she cannot but follow and serve Him.

After hearing Jesus teach in John 6:60, many people said, 'This is a hard saying, who can listen to it?' And in verse 66 we are told that 'After this many of his disciples turned back and no longer walked with him.' They were almost-believers. And then the Lord Jesus turned to the Twelve and said, 'Do you want to go away as well?' Simon Peter answered Him – in words that would not have sounded strange on the lips of Ruth the Moabitess – 'Lord, to whom shall we go? You have the words of eternal life.' Jesus Christ has the words of eternal life, and He asks those who follow Him, 'Do you want to go away as well? Will you also turn back? Or like Ruth, will you take me for your God and my people for your people?' Do you recognize with Simon Peter that there's nowhere else to go? However tempting and enticing the world may at times appear to you, however hard and painful following Jesus may be, there is nowhere else to go, for He alone has the words of eternal life.

Throughout the remainder of the book, Ruth is still repeatedly called 'Ruth the Moabite'. She can never quite get out from under that label. Deuteronomy 23:3 forbade Moabites entry to the congregation of Israel for ten generations. But it is 'Ruth the Moabite,' not yet Naomi the Hebrew, and not Orpah the other Moabite girl – it's 'Ruth the Moabite', the excluded outsider, who comes all the way in, and receives the Lord as her God. Isn't that the glory of the gospel? There is room for you under the shadow of the wings of the Almighty. There need be no Orpahs. There's room for all to come, like Ruth, and take the God of Israel, the God of covenant mercy, for your God as He is offered to you in Jesus Christ.

3. Naomi: The Backslidden Believer

It seems clear that Naomi knows the Lord. That much is evident by her benediction in verse 8: 'May the LORD deal kindly with you as you have dealt kindly with the dead and with me.' The word she uses, 'deal kindly,' is the word *hesed*. It means covenant love and mercy. It's the distinctive mark of the relationship between God and His people. God shows *hesed* to His children. The New Testament equivalent is *grace*. God gives grace to His people, binding Himself to them, and they to Him. And that is what Naomi pronounces upon her daughters-in-law here as she sends them home. It sounds very pious. But the benediction starts to ring hollow in light of her constant push to turn these girls away from God and His people, and her outright recommendation to Ruth that the gods of Moab might be her best bet. It all betrays the tragic story of a heart in dramatic spiritual decline.

And in verse 13 we get a glimpse of what drives her condition. When Orpah and Ruth protested at being turned back, Naomi replied, 'No, my daughters. It is exceedingly bitter to me for your sake that the hand of the LORD has gone out against me.' Here's how she reads her circumstances. Cleary, she believes in the sovereignty of God. She's perfectly orthodox on that point. But it's equally clear that she can no longer accept that the sovereign God is also good. That's what accounts for her response when the women of Bethlehem rush out to meet her upon her arrival:

> Do not call me, Naomi, (which means pleasant), call me Mara, (which means bitter), for the Almighty has dealt very bitterly with me. I went away full, and the LORD has brought me back empty. Why call me Naomi, when the LORD has testified against me, and the Almighty has brought calamity upon me?

There is not a Christian in this world who does not suffer at some point in their lives. But how careful we should be when suffering comes, that it does not do in us what it did in Naomi. It can cause a seed of bitterness towards God to germinate in our souls, when in fact, in God's design, it has always been intended to draw us closer to Him. Naomi is a soul in despair. She feels that God is somehow out to get her. She can see providence clearly enough, but she cannot see grace. All she knows at that moment is hurt and pain. The language she uses is very close to Job's, the righteous sufferer who sues God for justice. Like Job, Naomi thinks herself innocent, and God unjust. She's complaining that God has been overly severe, but she misreads God's hand in her sorrows, as we do too so very often. What she sees, however, as arbitrary and harsh as she wallows in the bitterness of her grief, the author of the book of Ruth wants us to begin to see quite differently. Here is a woman who has drifted far from the Lord. But notice, just as she has made the journey home, embittered and bereft, God is at work for good. There is a hint of His brighter design in verse 22: 'And they came to Bethlehem at the beginning of the barley harvest.' It's an adumbration of hope, a hint that a season of divine rebuke has almost passed. We are being taught to say, in the words of Cowper's hymn:

> Ye fearful saints, fresh courage take;
> The clouds ye so much dread,
> Are big with mercy, and shall break
> In blessings on your head.
>
> His purposes shall ripen fast,
> Unfolding every hour;
> The bud may have a bitter taste,
> But sweet will be the flower.[4]

As we scan back over the ways our hearts have dealt with suffering, aren't we being summoned by the ugly spectacle of Naomi's backslidden, bitter heart, not to rush so quickly to judgment on the Lord, who has ordained our trials? Instead, are we not being invited to do what so far only Ruth does? As she surveys her losses and crosses in meekness, she teaches us to kiss the hand that afflicts us, and to say with Job, 'The LORD gave, and the LORD has taken away, blessed be the name of the LORD' (Job 1:21) Those who learn well the lessons that sore providences teach say with the Psalmist, 'It was good

---

4. William Cowper, *God Moves in a Mysterious Way*, 1774, Trinity Hymnal (Philadelphia: Great Commission Publications, ©1990), p. 128.

for me that I was afflicted, that I might learn your statutes' (Ps. 119:71). God is teaching and training us in our trials, and He purposes our good in and through our griefs.

Orpah was an almost-believer. She started well but did not finish. What about you? Perhaps you too have started well. Will you cross the finish line? Or will you turn back, as you count the cost of following Jesus?

Ruth was a new believer. She clung to the Lord and took His covenant as her own. Perhaps the Lord is calling you, just like He called Ruth, to come to Him and find refuge under the wings of the Almighty. Don't turn back to Moab. Turn to the Lord Jesus Christ, and come to take refuge under the shadow of His wings.

Naomi was a backslidden believer. Her heart was consumed with bitterness. Maybe that's you. Maybe you're still far away. And yet, could it not be the case that, in all your sufferings, God has been at work to bring you back to Himself? We need to learn in our trials not to judge the Lord 'by feeble sense, but trust him for his grace,' because the truth is, that 'behind a frowning providence' He does indeed 'hide a smiling face'.

3

The Way Ahead
(Ruth 2)

Who is the main character in the book of Ruth? A correct answer to that question is vital if we are going to understand its message. Is it Naomi, perhaps? She certainly seems to take center stage in the opening chapter at least. Or how about Ruth? Very quickly the storyline begins to swirl around her, to be sure. Or maybe you'd suggest Boaz? He is introduced to us here in chapter 2 for the first time, and he'll be the one by whose agency all the tensions of the story will resolve. Who would you say is the main character in the book of Ruth?

It's not Naomi, not Ruth, not even Boaz: the main character in the book of Ruth is the only Person who has no direct dialogue dedicated to Him. He never speaks. In fact, He stays in the background throughout. The main character in the book of Ruth is the Lord God Himself. And the author of Ruth points us to Him, albeit rather furtively and subtly at times, over and over again. If read as a romance, we will miss the point. If read as a morality tale – cautioning us about good and bad behavior – we will misconstrue the message. Read it correctly, and we will learn to trace the often oblique ways in which the fate of Naomi and Ruth reveals the handiwork of the Lord.

Of course, the book of Ruth aims at much more in us than the development of literary skill learned through a close reading of the biblical text. The book of Ruth aims at the cultivation of a spiritual skill, taught by the biblical text to be sure, but practiced in the details of our daily lives. Learning to read God's workmanship in the mundane particulars of this story is meant to help us see His fingerprints in our own circumstances also. In other words, God is not just the main character in the text before us; He is also the main character in the storyline of your life. Your life, no less than the book of Ruth, is all about Him. 'For from him, and through him and to him are all things, to whom be the glory forever Amen.' (Rom. 11:36 NKJV).

So God is the main character in the book of Ruth, and as we turn our attention to Ruth chapter 2, we are going to see three lessons about His ways and works.

1. The Providence of God

Things have gone terribly wrong for the family of Naomi. Her husband and two sons are dead. Orpah, her daughter-in-law, has deserted her and turned back to her pagan ways in the land of Moab. And now Naomi and her other daughter-in-law, Ruth, are destitute and extremely vulnerable. While Ruth responded to the suffering and losses of their situation in faith, Naomi was filled with bitterness.

But there are two notes of hope that sound clearly above the minor chords of Naomi's suffering. First, as we have seen, in 1:22 they return to Bethlehem 'at the beginning of barley harvest'. And secondly, in 2:1, Naomi has 'a relative of her husband's, a worthy man of the clan of Elimelech.' The first informs us that these two bedraggled and forlorn women arrive home sometime in mid to late April after the rainy season has ended. The food was plentiful, and times were now good in Judah. The famine, that was a mark of divine rebuke for sin, is over, and there seems to be a spiritual awakening going on among the people.

Notice the remarkable greetings exchanged between the field laborers and Boaz in verse 4: 'The LORD be with you.' Boaz calls. And they respond, 'The LORD bless you.' The typical greeting was 'Shalom', our equivalent of 'Hello, how are you doing?' But that's not how these rough, working men respond to Boaz. Their words echo the Aaronic blessing in Numbers 6. There is something unusual about life in

Bethlehem in these days: hard, working men are quoting scripture to one another and invoking the covenant name of the LORD in the ordinary course of their labor. These are men with calluses on their hands. They are rough farmhands out in the fields and here they are quoting scripture to each other in the regular business of a day's toil. The beginning of the barley harvest seems to signal the beginning of a real spiritual awakening in the hearts of God's people. That's the first hopeful note in the text as Naomi and Ruth finally return home to Bethlehem.

The second note tells us that, although Naomi can see no way of supplying a husband for Ruth, the narrator certainly can. As it turns out there is one who stands in the legal position to be able to fulfill the obligations of the levirate laws that applied in these circumstances. There is a near relative who can replace Ruth's dead husband and carry on the family line and preserve the family's allotment in the land. Clearly, we are being set up by the author, aren't we? The ball is on the tee, and we are left waiting for the swing. We can see what neither Naomi nor Ruth know quite yet. Naomi had said, 'I went away full, but the LORD has brought be back empty.' But we know now that the means to fill her emptiness to overflowing are already in place in the marvelous providence of God.

Now, the book of Ruth is a master-class in Hebrew story-telling. Having shown us these hopeful indicators, the narrator then quite purposefully leaves us hanging, waiting for the plot to develop, before we discover just how it is that the abundance of grain and the intriguing figure of Boaz will finally intersect with the hapless Naomi and Ruth. He has a knowing smile already playing on his face as he hints to us at what is to come: 'The anticipation is building. God is at work. Just wait and see.' That's the message. And then, with the stage at last carefully set, the dialogue begins. Look at it. Ruth asks permission of her mother-in-law Naomi to go and glean in the fields: 'Let me go to the field and glean among the ears of grain after him in whose sight I shall find favor.' She is availing herself of the provision of Deuteronomy 24:19-22:

> When you reap your harvest in your field and forget a sheaf in the field, you shall not go back to get it. It shall be for the

sojourner, the fatherless, and the widow, that the LORD your
God may bless you in all the work of your hands... You shall
remember that you were a slave in the land of Egypt; therefore,
I command you to do this.

Under Moses, God had rescued and redeemed Israel from
Egyptian bondage, where no one made provision for them
in their misery and poverty. They were strangers in a strange
land themselves once, and there they had no such provision
of mercy. And so, because God had mercy on them, from then
on, His people were to have mercy on the poor and the needy,
the foreigner, the fatherless and the widow – in short, on
people just like Ruth. So she is making use of the legal rights
given to her in God's law. And yet she also clearly knows
that her heritage as a Moabitess marked her as a particularly
unwelcome visitor in Bethlehem. And so, whatever the law
said, if she's going to find a place to glean that day, it would
have to be because of the unusual generosity and kindness
of the harvesters. Deuteronomy 24 makes provision for the
poor, for someone like Ruth to come and glean. Deuteronomy
23:3, however, is the place where Moabites are excluded
from the congregation of Israel for ten generations. So Ruth
knows that she's in a real bind. She knows she has the legal
right to glean, but she also knows that she is an outcast. She
is a stranger, and alien within Israel's gates. So, will she be
allowed to glean or not?

And as we read verse 3 to find out, it's hard not to picture
the knowing wink the author throws our way. Having
received permission from her mother-in-law, Ruth 'set out
and went and gleaned in the field after the reapers, and
she happened to come to the part of the field belonging to
Boaz, who was of the clan of Elimelech.' The Hebrew of the
passage is particularly emphatic as it highlights the apparent
coincidence. It says something like 'the chance that chanced
upon her was that she came to glean in Boaz' field'. 'The
happenstance that happened to her.' 'What a stroke of luck.'
'Would you believe it?' That's what the author is saying.

Think for a moment about the chain of circumstances that
all had to align for this coincidence to occur. Ruth and Naomi
had to arrive at the right time for the barley harvest. Ruth had

to land in the field of Boaz. And look at verse 4. While Ruth is working in the field, who should happen to stop by but Boaz himself. The timing of this is breathtaking. And it is set in deliberate contrast to the commentary Naomi provides on the sovereignty of God in the previous chapter. In the bitterness of her grief, to Naomi, God is all sovereignty, but no goodness. He is all power, but no mercy. He is the Almighty, to be sure, but He is also arbitrary and unjust. That's how Naomi reads things. But here, as Chapter 2 opens, we get to see the truth. However, Naomi understands the situation, God is at work in the details of their lives for good.

A mathematician and meteorologist named Edward Lorenz worked on the development of computer models designed to map and predict weather patterns. He discovered that when he ran his data with tiny, statistically inconsequential variations at the initial stages of weather development, it produced dramatically different results compared to when he ran the same data without those variations. Rounding out the numbers and discarding the minuscule variables, the results at the end, quite unexpectedly, varied remarkably. These tiny, seemingly inconsequential data points created factors that led, as the model played out, to massive differences in weather-outcomes. Lorenz went on to illustrate his discovery by coining the now famous metaphor of a butterfly flapping its wings, creating minuscule fluctuations in atmospheric conditions. Weeks later, those tiny variables created by the butterfly's wings contribute to conditions that led to the formation of a massive hurricane. His point was this: the smallest things sometimes have seismic implications.

And that is precisely the lesson of this first part of the chapter. The seemingly random decision to glean in this particular field, at this particular time, on this particular day, will prove to have long-term significance for the future welfare of Naomi and Ruth that neither could have anticipated. The reason? God is sovereign and works all things according to the counsel of His will, to the praise of His glorious grace. The truth is, there are no insignificant actions, no throwaway moments. And that is the great adventure of the Christian life. We know that our times are in God's hands. We know that 'in God's book were written, every one' of the days 'that were formed for' us 'when as yet there were none of them' (Ps. 139:16). We know that God is 'working his purposes out as year succeeds to year', and so we know that even seemingly random things, even the happenstances that happen to us, may prove to have significance for the glory of God and the good of His people that we could never have imagined.

That is a precious truth full of comfort, perhaps especially when we struggle with questions of guidance, as Christians often do. We try to anticipate what is going to happen. We worry about tomorrow and are unsure what we need to do next. We plan and strategize, but the future is out of our control. So we stress and fret over how to be prepared. We often don't know what to do for the best. And it's exactly here that Ruth's example is so enormously helpful. She and Naomi don't know how they will survive long-term. They've come back to the land, sure enough, but so far things are no better here than they were in Moab.

But Ruth, the new believer, does the next thing. She can't see a year down the line. She can't even see tomorrow. So she simply does the next thing. She follows the pattern laid out in the Word of God, in Deuteronomy 24, for the destitute widow and the sojourner in the land. She has no access to new revelation telling her about tomorrow and the day after, and the day after that, so she follows the course the Scriptures indicate. She does the next thing that she knows to do in faithful obedience to the clear precepts of Holy Scripture. And the sovereign God, into whose hands she has entrusted her life, overrules her desperate situation and guides her steps.

That's the secret, you know, of Christian contentment. You do not need to know about tomorrow and next week and six months from now and ten years from now. You need to know what God would have you do today, how He would have you live today. Attend to the clear guidance of the Scriptures. Study the glory of God and the good of others. Do your duty today and trust the whole weight of tomorrow into the hands of the God who governs all things in sovereign grace for the good of those who love Him. It was living in precisely that stance of dependent trust that enabled the apostle Paul to say, 'I have learned in whatever situation I am to be content. I know how to be brought low and I know how to abound. In any and every circumstance I have learned the secret of facing plenty and hunger, abundance and need. I can do all things through him who strengthens me' (Phil. 4:11-13). That was Ruth's stance too. Trust the providence of God for tomorrow, and do the next thing in quiet faith today.

2. The Provision of God

In verse 4 Boaz arrives in the field and greets his men. He is described in verse 1 as 'a worthy man'. That's not a great translation. The same description is used for example, of Gideon in Judges 6:12, where it is translated 'a mighty man of valor', or 'warrior'. Boaz however, unlike Gideon, is not depicted as a hero in the book of Ruth because of his military skills. Neither is he a hero because of his standing and honor in the community, as the phrase is sometimes translated. No, Boaz is a great man supremely because of his character. He shows up for work in verse 4, and the first words from his lips, the very first words recorded in scripture coming from Boaz' mouth, invoke the name and blessing of Almighty God. Here is a hero indeed, worthy of emulation.

And as he talks with his foreman, there is a young woman in the field, laboring among the other women and following behind the reapers, who immediately catches his eye. 'She's the Moabitess everyone's been talking about; the one who came back with Naomi. She asked to glean in the field,' the foreman says, 'and I gave permission, and she hasn't stopped since morning. She's been at it all day.' Apparently, Ruth, no less than Boaz, is a person of character, and Boaz is impressed, and he resolves to do something for her good. In verses 8 and 9 he tells her she need not glean anywhere else but in his field, neither should she be wary of going close behind the reapers as they work. He has undertaken to ensure her safety in a rough working environment. She should feel free to drink the water the young men had drawn for the laborers without any restriction. He is treating her as though she were a member of his own household. And then later that evening Boaz included Ruth among his laborers in the evening meal. And when she was out of earshot, in verse 15, he gave instructions to 'Let her glean even among the sheaves and do not reproach her. And also pull out some from the bundles for her and leave it for her to glean, and do not rebuke her.' There is now a positive conspiracy developing to provide more for her than ever she could have gathered otherwise.

And if you will look at the exchange that takes place between Boaz and Ruth in verses 10-13 you will see the key to understanding the significance of all of that. More is going on than Boaz trying to impress a pretty girl. In verse 10 Ruth is quite overcome at the kindness she's been shown. Notice her reaction. She prostrates herself before Boaz and cries out, 'Why have I found favor in your eyes, that you should take notice of me since I am a foreigner?' She had set out that morning no doubt with some slim hopes that maybe she might be allowed to pick at the edges of someone's field here and there, and eke out just enough to scrape by for the day. She never thought to be treated with this sort of kindness and consideration. And in his response, Boaz explains why he had been so generous to her. He has heard of her commitment to her mother-in-law in the face of great tragedy. He knows all about how she has left everything – her land and her people – to come to a people she does not know. And he pronounces his benediction upon her: 'The Lord repay you for what you have done, and a full reward be given you by the Lord, the God of Israel, under whose wings you have come to take refuge.'

Ruth has come to take refuge under the wings of the Almighty. She has placed all her hope and trust in God. She has ventured everything, staked her entire future and destiny, upon God and His grace. And Boaz resolves not merely to *speak* a blessing, but to *be* a blessing; not merely to be the *spokesman* of God's covenant mercy, but to be himself the *agent* of it. And so, when the day is done, in verse 17, we discover that Ruth has gathered an ephah of barley. That is almost too much for one person to carry. She comes staggering home after her first day gleaning, to the utter amazement of her mother-in-law. Far beyond Ruth's hopes and expectations, and quite contrary to Naomi's bitter view of God, the Lord has provided more, extravagantly more, than they needed.

Now Boaz, this man of godly character, as we will see with ever-growing clarity as the story develops, is a picture of the Lord Jesus Christ. And that is as true at this moment in the story as anywhere else. When we come to take refuge under the wings of the Almighty, a greater than Boaz does more than speak empty benedictions to us in response. He is the One by whom more grace flows to us than we have need. That's what happened to Ruth with Boaz. It's what happens more wonderfully and fully to us, with Jesus Christ. In Matthew 14, remember, some five thousand souls attended Jesus' ministry and needed to be fed. All that was at hand were five loaves and two fish. But Jesus did not turn the needy people away. He multiplied the resources to supply the need, with twelve baskets of leftovers once everyone had eaten their fill. Jesus does not turn the needy away.

The same God who made provision for the orphans and the widows and the sojourners to glean in Israel's fields has made provision for you, in His Son Jesus Christ. No-one who ever came in faith to Christ empty, went away empty still. In fact, the lesson of Ruth's ephah of grain, like the lesson of Jesus' twelve baskets of leftovers, is more wonderful than that. It is not just that there is grace to fill your deepest spiritual need, under the wings of the Almighty. It is not just that Jesus is an *adequate* Savior for every sinner who seeks Him. No. It is that there is more grace than you can manage, more grace than you can exhaust, more grace in Christ – an extravagance of grace in Him – for you. There is super-abounding provision for you in the God of mercy and grace in Jesus Christ. Some of us live in fear as we face tomorrow because deep down we are not sure if Jesus is up to the task of supplying our deep heart-needs. We are not entirely sure if we can trust Christ to provide. But, as Ruth staggered home under the enormous weight of barley, I'm sure she would tell you, albeit between grunts of exertion, that He *can* provide, and He *will* provide. There is more grace in Him than need in you, and you will never exhaust the provision of God.

3. The Pursuit of God

So, Ruth comes staggering home. And you can see Naomi's eyes get big as she asks in amazement, 'Where did you glean today? And where have you worked? Blessed be the man who took notice of you.' In her backslidden, bitter-hearted state, she is altogether unprepared for this sort of kindness.

And when Ruth tells her she had been working in Boaz' field, a calculating new light begins to gleam in her mother-in-law's eyes. And an idea leaps suddenly into her mind. Look at verse 20, 'May he be blessed by the LORD, whose kindness has not forsaken the living or the dead. The man is a close relative of ours, one of our redeemers.' The word for close relative is *go'el*, a kinsman-redeemer, one who can fulfill the stipulations of the levirate law, provide a substitute for the dead husband, and prolong the family line and preserve the family lands. 'Keep gleaning in his field,' she tells Ruth, 'and let's see where this goes.'

Clearly, Naomi thinks to play matchmaker. All of a sudden, she has a wonderful plan for Ruth's and Boaz' lives. But as she sets out to gerrymander a romance between her daughter-in-law and Boaz, her kinsman-redeemer, do not miss how God has also been pursuing Naomi's wayward heart all along. Did you catch the change of tone in Naomi's voice in verse 20? When last she spoke of the LORD, back in 1:20-21, He was the one who had embittered her heart and brought her home empty. He was responsible for the calamity that had befallen her. But here now she seems to see things differently: 'the kindness of the LORD' – the divine *hesed* – the saving, covenant mercy of the LORD – 'has not forsaken the living or the dead.' Now, suddenly, she sees the hand of God at work in grace. At long last she notices kindness where before she saw only calamity. Naomi sets out to help Ruth win Boaz's heart, not realizing that the God of covenant mercy had set out to win Naomi's heart for Himself. Thomas Watson, the great Puritan, once said that 'grace dissolves and liquefies the soul, causing a spiritual thaw.'[1] That is what appears to have happened in Naomi's heart, at last. There is a spiritual thaw, as the warmth of the divine *hesed* – the kindness, and grace of God – begins to seep through her sorrow and melt her heart.

The Great Seeker, the Great Pursuer, of the affection and devotion of your heart is God Himself. He isn't interested in mere lip-service, but neither is He put off by your backsliding. 'The Father,' Jesus says in John 4, is 'seeking true

---

1. Thomas Watson, *The Godly Man's Picture* (Edinburgh, UK: Banner of Truth, 1992), p. 55.

worshippers'. He is in hot-pursuit of your heart. You may have drifted far away. Some of you may even have allowed bitterness to creep in, in the midst of suffering, to poison your trust in Jesus. But the Lord, who has not stopped showing kindness to the living and the dead, wants your heart for Himself. He is working with you, speaking to you, calling you in His Word even now to come back to Him. He wants to start a spiritual thaw in your soul. I wonder how you will answer His overtures of mercy.

The providence of God – you know you can trust His sovereignty. The provision of God – there's abundant grace for you in Christ. And the pursuit of God – He wants your heart for Himself. Won't you come back to Him?

4

The Wrong Turn?
(Ruth 3)

The third chapter of Ruth is without a doubt the most challenging one in the book. As you start to read, very quickly it looks like a terrible wrong turn is about to be made in Naomi and Ruth's spiritual journey – the consequences of which could be calamitous. But it's also, arguably, the most helpful chapter in the book of Ruth. It is filled with moral ambiguities, to be sure, but it's also filled with insights into the complexities and contradictions of even the redeemed human heart. It shows us ourselves, and it overflows with intimations of God's sovereign mercy, that superintends even our missteps for His glory and our good. In the end, as we will see, it leads us to the gospel of grace.

And one of the ways that we'll begin to see that is so is to pay attention to the cinematography. A great movie director will often craft a scene with visual cues that serve to clue us into the director's agenda. And that is precisely how the author of the book of Ruth is operating here. Pay attention to the cinematography. In our chapter, for example, you will notice that the action takes place in three scenes, each taking place at different times of the day. In verses 1-5, the opening dialogue between Naomi and Ruth happens probably in the late afternoon, after Ruth has come home from the day's gleaning, just as the sun begins to wane. Then in verses 6-13, the central section of the chapter plays out during the dark hours of the night, once Boaz has fallen asleep on the threshing floor. And then, the last scene, in 14-18, tells us what happened as the sun came up the next morning.

Pay attention to the cinematography, and you will begin to understand something of the significance of what is taking place. So here, as we watch the late afternoon shadows gather, in the first part of the chapter, as Naomi shares her plan to secure Boaz for Ruth as her new husband, we begin to feel more than a little foreboding. This doesn't read like a wise plan at all. What is Naomi thinking? And then, we follow Ruth down onto the threshing floor that night and the tension mounts. The scary cello music begins to play. This is a very dangerous moment, fraught with spiritual tension and moral alarm. And by now we have our hands over our eyes, barely able to watch. Is this really going to be as bad as it looks? But then finally, as the sun comes up at long last, there is a palpable sense of relief – and we remember once more that Boaz really is a man of God, that Ruth really is a young woman of integrity, and God really cannot be out-maneuvered, not even by the Machiavellian schemes of a matchmaking mother-in-law.

1. The persistence of sin in a believing heart

The last verse of chapter 2 explains that the barley and wheat harvests are now over, which tells us it had been several months now since the idea first occurred to Naomi that Boaz might be the very man to rescue them from their destitution. Full of new hope, Naomi's advice had been that Ruth should keep close to Boaz and his young women 'and let's see where this thing goes.' But now, months later, instead of a husband for Ruth, all they had to show for it was plenty of grain. But Naomi is undeterred.

Notice her words to Ruth, in verse 1: 'My daughter, should I not seek rest for you that it may be well with you?' In Judges 3:11, or 3:30, or 5:31 or 8:28, during the period within which the events of the book of Ruth took place, we learn that when Israel stayed faithful to the Lord, the Lord gave the land rest. And that is what Naomi wants for Ruth: rest, security, peace. And verse 2 tells us that Naomi knows that in God's law there was a mechanism that made provision for precisely that eventuality: 'Is not Boaz our relative with whose young women you were?' Boaz, Naomi is hinting, stands in a position to substitute for Ruth's dead husband, and so preserve the family line and inheritance in the land. Clearly, Naomi loves Ruth and wants to provide for her. That's her motive. It's important we see that so that we're not too hard on Naomi. Her motives are good. But then, look at verses 2-5. Whatever her motives Naomi seems to have grown impatient, and so she decides to give poor Boaz a not-so-subtle nudge in the right direction.

> See, he is winnowing barley tonight at the threshing floor. Wash therefore and anoint yourself, and put on your cloak and go down to the threshing floor, but do not make yourself known to the man until he has finished eating and drinking. But when he lies down, observe the place where he lies. Then go and uncover his feet and lie down, and he will tell you what to do (3:2-4).

Now, no matter which way we look at it, that is a distressing piece of counsel. Some commentators read Naomi's words as instructions, in effect, to dress for seduction. 'Put on your prettiest dress and some fine perfume. Get all dressed up, Ruth, and go get yourself a husband.' Tempting as that interpretation may seem, I really think it's an over-reading of the text. Much more plausible is the suggestion that Ruth has thus far been dressed in the ritual garments of a mourning widow. Perhaps Naomi thinks the reason that Boaz has kept his distance these past few months is out of respect for Ruth's grief. And so, by washing and perfuming herself and putting on her cloak, she was dressing, not for seduction, but simply to signal to Boaz that her mourning was over. If he was at all interested, she wanted him to know that he need not keep his distance any longer.

But even so, the fact still remains that Naomi's advice to Ruth was fraught with moral danger. Twice in chapter 2 – first in 2:9 on the lips of Boaz, and then once in 2:22 on the lips of Naomi herself – we were told of the potential for Ruth to be assaulted by the young men who worked the harvest. And yet now, suddenly, driven by her impatience with God's timing, we hear this same Naomi sending her young, single,

vulnerable daughter-in-law down to the threshing floor to
spend the night alone with Boaz. Add to that Hosea 9:1, which
tells us that prostitutes used the threshing floor at harvest
time, and the scene grows even more alarming, doesn't it?
Add to that still further the parallels between this part of the
chapter and the story of Genesis 19, and our spiritual alarm
bells ought all to be ringing loud and clear.

In Genesis 19, Lot's two daughters have incestuous
relations with their drunken father. The firstborn child from
that union was named Moab, Ruth's direct ancestor. Perhaps
Naomi assumed that, given the right circumstances, Ruth
would simply revert to type, her newfound faith in Israel's
God notwithstanding? Did she think that the Moabite in her
would shine through in the end anyway, 'so why not make
use of it while there was still time and secure a husband
along the way?' But while her plan seems to require Ruth
the Moabitess to revert to type and repeat the sexual sin with
which the name of Moab had become synonymous, in the
end, it's really *Naomi*, not Ruth, who bears the stamp of Moab
most clearly. What's the lesson here? Isn't it that you can take
the child of God out of Moab, but it's not nearly so easy to get
Moab out of the child of God?

Frankly, Naomi's counsel to Ruth here reads like the advice
of an unbeliever. It is hardly the godly counsel of a believing
parent. And yet, as a pastor, I wish I could say that Naomi was
an isolated case. Over and over again I have sat with young
couples who profess faith in Jesus and who are planning to
get married, and when I ask, they no longer even so much as
blush to tell me that they are already sleeping together. 'Of
course. Why wouldn't we be?' That's their response. There's
plenty of Moab about them, their profession of faith in Jesus
notwithstanding. Or another example: in a previous church
we had a wonderful woman who served as a counselor at a
Christian crisis pregnancy center. 'You'd be surprised,' she
said, 'how often young girls come to us in significant distress
because their Christian mothers were pressuring them to get
an abortion.' Mom wanted a college experience for her little
girl, you see.

Don't think that because you've come back to Bethlehem,
that Moab can no longer rear its ugly head in your life. Do

not think, because you have become a Christian, that sin may no longer suddenly flare up with renewed vigor and force, when all had seemed so quiet for so long. Sin may sometimes slumber long and appear quite subdued in our hearts and we may have many small victories along the way. But temptation always waits to strike until we are least on guard and most at ease. Let's use Naomi's example to provoke us to watch and pray, lest we fall into temptation, because the truth is, our spirits may be willing but our flesh is weak. You remember Paul's confession in Romans 7:19? 'I do not do the good I want, but the evil I do not want is what I keep on doing… I find it to be a law that when I want to do right, evil lies close at hand…' Be on your guard, believer in Jesus. When you want to do right, evil lies close at hand. 'Sin crouches at the door. Its desire is for you, but you must rule over it.' (Gen. 4:7). God may have brought you out of Moab by His grace, but it takes a lifetime to get Moab out of you. Therefore, be on guard and do not think that because you have come to know Jesus you may let your guard down in your battle with sin. The persistence of sin in a believing heart.

2. The Good News of Rest for a Restless Heart

As the sun set in verse 6, Ruth was watching from the shadows. When Boaz finally threw himself down next to the grain that was piled high on the threshing floor, she crept forward, uncovered his feet, and lay down, just as her mother-in-law had advised. And then, 'at midnight the man was startled (well, wouldn't you be with your feet sticking out of bed like this.). And he turned over, and behold, a woman lay at his feet. And he said, "Who are you?"' (v. 8). It is really a mark of the godliness of the man that that's all he said. What a fright the poor fellow must have gotten. And while Boaz wiped the sleep from his eyes and the drool from his chin and tried to flatten his bed-head hair, Ruth seized the initiative: 'I am Ruth, your servant. Spread your wings over your servant, for you are a redeemer' (v. 9).

Now that's not in the script. She wasn't supposed to say that. But as it turns out, Ruth has better moral instincts than Naomi at this point. Actually, the phrase 'spread your wings over your servant' is a double-entendre. It can also be translated as 'spread the corner of your garment over me'. Now, again, we need to be clear, she's not trying to seduce Boaz. But she is proposing marriage to him. This is a euphemism for marriage in the Hebrew Bible. God Himself uses it metaphorically to describe His covenant with Israel as a betrothal in Ezekiel 16:8, for example. As one scholar put it, this language signifies 'the establishment of a new relationship and the symbolic declaration of the husband to provide for the sustenance of the future wife'.[1] That's what she is asking for here.

And just to add to the drama and the romance of the moment, by framing her proposal in these specific terms she is quoting words from the first time she and Boaz met, all those months before. Isn't that beautiful? Back in 2:12 Boaz had said that Ruth had come to take refuge 'under the wings of the LORD'. And now she says to Boaz, 'Spread your wings over your servant.' You see what she is really asking? She is saying that one of the ways the LORD will spread His wings over her in His covenant love is by Boaz spreading his wings over her in the covenant of marriage. And notice that she presses that upon him as a duty, in verse 9: 'You are a redeemer.' 'You are a *go'el*. You are one of those men who can fill the role vacated by my dead husband, according to the Law of Moses. You are qualified to rescue me, Boaz.' That's what she says.

Now one can't help feeling sorry for Boaz at this point. After all, this has to be a lot to take in in the middle of the night with a strange woman looming at you out of the shadows. And it's not hard to imagine how Ruth must have been feeling at this point either. She's made her speech and taken a huge risk. She has made herself extremely vulnerable. And now, as she waits for Boaz' reply, everything hangs by a thread. He might have taken advantage of her. He might have rebuked her and publicly shamed her. Everything hangs on Boaz' reply. What a relief, then, when he deals with her with consummate gentleness and godly care. Notice how he replies. First, he blesses her and interprets her interest in him

---

1. Cited in Daniel I. Block, *Judges, Ruth* (Nashville, TN: Broadman and Holman, 1999), p. 691.

as an act of *hesed*, covenant love towards him. She could have gone after younger, richer, stronger men. But she wants him. And then he tells her that he will do for her what she asks. Her heart must have leapt for joy at this point. Instead of disaster, God, it seems, is richly blessing Ruth. It's wonderful.

And yet, right at this point, just as our hearts are leaping, suddenly, a new note of tension is introduced: 'There is a redeemer closer than I' (v. 12). There is someone else, unknown to both Naomi and Ruth, who is a closer relative to Elimelech than Boaz, and he has a prior responsibility and claim. Nevertheless, Boaz is a godly man who cares for Ruth and he will take care of the matter as soon as the sun rises. 'If the other man will not redeem, then,' says Boaz with a solemn oath, 'as the LORD lives, I will redeem you.'

Throughout that long restless night, Ruth has risked everything in pursuit of rest. That was what Naomi wanted for her back in verse 1: *rest*. And now, at last, Boaz has committed himself, one way or another, to ensuring that Ruth and Naomi find it. It would be a profitable study at this point to spend time meditating on Boaz's godliness in the face of sexual temptation. And there is certainly a reminder to us here that whatever checks and balances we put in place, whatever accountability we may have to help us stay pure, temptation will always find its way in, like water finding the cracks in any surface. And in those moments, our last defense has to be the pattern of faithful obedience to God that we have consistently accumulated in times when temptation has not assailed us, so that when it does, there is a kind of spiritual muscle memory, and we react not with lust but with holiness. The last defense of the heart against sin is a pattern and habit of obedience that holds firm when temptation comes.

It would be equally profitable to remark at length upon Ruth at this point. In the Hebrew ordering of the books of the Bible, Ruth follows immediately after the book of Proverbs, which ends with a description of the woman of noble character. Proverbs 31:31 says of her that 'her works praise her in the gates', which is actually the same phrase Boaz uses in Ruth 3:11, translated as 'all the townsmen know that you are a worthy woman'. Literally he says, 'All the gates of my people know that you are a worthy woman.' Ruth is the embodiment of a Proverbs 31 woman. She is a woman who models for us godly courage and a determination to live like a true Israelite, a true child of God, even when Naomi acts like a Moabitess.

But are we stretching things too far to dwell for a moment on Boaz' words to Ruth, that strike a new note of uncertainty in her heart? When he told her that '[t]here is a redeemer closer than I', he meant only that there is someone nearer by blood to Elimelech than he. This closer redeemer must be given the right to act first. But when read against the big idea of the book of Ruth as a whole, it is hard to resist the temptation to hear an irony in Boaz' words, because when the story ends, and all is settled at last, we are left to conclude that there is indeed a redeemer closer than Boaz. He is the Lord of covenant love Himself. It has been the Lord who has worked all along to woo and win the hearts of both Naomi and Ruth, and to weave them into the fabric of the grand tapestry of redemptive history, that through them the true and final *go'el*, the perfect Redeemer, and Boaz' descendant and heir, the Lord Jesus Christ, might come to give us all the rest we seek. Remember St. Augustine's prayer: 'Thou hast made us for thyself, and our hearts are restless till they find their rest in thee.' You may be restless at the moment, and you always will be restless until you find rest in your true kinsman Redeemer, the Lord Jesus Christ. 'Come to me, all you who are weary and heavy laden,' He cries, 'and I will give you rest.' There's rest for you in Jesus. Go to Him.

3. The Promise of Fullness for an Empty Heart

At last the morning dawns. Boaz, because he's a man of God, makes sure no-one finds out that Ruth had spent the night there. He is a good man and he wants to protect her reputation. Love, after all, covers a multitude of wrongs. And then he tells Ruth to bring her cloak and he will fill it with grain. Six measures of barley are what he gives her. It's an enormous amount, an almost ridiculous amount. She has to have Boaz help her lift it onto her back (v. 15). She staggers back to her mother-in-law, doubtless red-faced and out of breath. And Naomi's question in verse 16 tells us that she can see immediately that Ruth has changed. She asks, 'How did you fare my daughter?' In the Hebrew, that's actually the same question that Boaz asked her in the middle of the night. Literally, she asked, 'Who *are you*, my daughter?' Can you really be the same Ruth this morning that left my house last night? Something dramatic has happened to you. That's the sentiment of her question. And in answer Ruth dumps the grain on the floor, and between gasps, reports Boaz's words.

And notice carefully the punch line. It has been held over from his speech on the threshing floor the night before, for this very moment. 'Boaz said to me, "You must not go back *to your mother-in-law* empty handed."' Your mother-in-law. It turns out Boaz has a pretty good read on Naomi's matchmaking after all, hasn't he? She thought she was so subtle. But Boaz has the measure of her. And he has chosen his message for the mother-in-law very carefully. Notice especially the phrase, 'empty-handed.' It was the same phrase Naomi used to describe what she felt God had done to her in the death of her husband and sons. 'I went away full,' she said, 'but have come back empty.'

He was saying in effect: 'Don't you understand, Naomi, that you really do not need to manipulate circumstances? You really can trust the LORD to provide.' The massive haul of barley was a visual aid, a kind of dramatized promise to that effect. Boaz will change not just Ruth but Naomi too, forever. 'You will no longer be empty. You *will* be full again.' And in the last line of the chapter, it seems that, at last, Naomi has got the message, hasn't she? She gives up her scheming. Her bitterness is gone. She is content, at long last, simply to wait and see. She will now trust Boaz, and trusting him, she will trust the LORD.

Do you worry about tomorrow? Has painful past experience made you fearful that the days ahead will be just as sore, so that now you struggle to trust the Lord at all? That had been Naomi's experience. She was empty. But the Lord was signaling to her that if she would but trust Him and His redeemer Boaz, her emptiness would be filled. There is no promise that hardship and sorrow or loss or pain will never again intrude into your life. But there *is* a promise that emptiness need never again characterize your heart. Jesus said in John 10:10, 'I have come that you might have life and life in abundance' (life to the full). He is greater than Boaz, and the great signal to you that He will deliver on His promise is no mere bundle of grain. It's the cross and the empty tomb. He gives, not a portion of the barley harvest for you, but Himself. 'If God is for us, who can be against us? He who did not spare his own Son, but gave him up for us all, how will he not also, along with him, graciously give us all things?' (Rom. 8:31-32). There is fullness for empty hearts in Jesus Christ, and there is rest for restless hearts in Jesus Christ, so that when the persistent sin that festers, even in believing hearts, rears its ugly head again, we may know where to turn in our time of need. We must turn to Jesus Christ, the Redeemer who is closest of all.

5

The Savior and So and So
(Ruth 4:1-12)

The congregation I served in London met in a beautiful old church building on Aldersgate Street. The churchyard adjacent to the church was converted into one of London's smallest and most beautiful public parks in the nineteenth century. It's called Postman's Park, because adjacent to the park on the other side was the old Royal Mail offices. Along the back wall of the park is a curious memorial. It features a covered porch, open on one side, with a wall covered in fifty-four Royal Doulton ceramic tiles. Each tile bears a simple memorial to ordinary citizens of the city who died saving the life of another.

Thomas Griffin

Fitters labourer

April 12, 1899

In a boiler explosion at a Battersea sugar refinery was fatally scalded in returning to search for his mate.

Walter Peart, Driver

And Harry Dean, Fireman

Of the Windsor Express

On July 18, 1898

Whilst being scalded and burnt sacrificed their lives in saving the train.

Elizabeth Boxall

Aged 17 of Bethnal Green

Who died of injuries received in trying to save a child from a runaway horse.

June 20, 1888

Alice Ayres

Daughter of a bricklayer's laborer

Who by intrepid conduct saved 3 children from a burning house in Union Street, Borough at the cost of her own young life.

April 24, 1885

And on and on the memorial goes, simply listing the bare facts of each case. I always found it to be quite moving to stand in the beauty of that delightful little park and read the catalog of names that have not been forgotten on account of their sacrifice.

There is a sense in which the fourth chapter of the book of Ruth is also all about names that are worthy of remembrance and, as we'll see, about names that are not worth remembering at all. In some ways, the great problem that the narrator has set out to resolve in the storyline of the book of Ruth is, 'How shall the name of Elimelech be preserved in Israel, now that he has no heir?' Naomi, his widow, can't bear him a son. Ruth, his daughter-in-law, has likewise lost her husband, Mahlon. And so Elimelech's name, and along with it, his allotment in the Promised Land, will surely be lost forever. To possess real estate in the Land of Promise that could be passed on to your heirs served as a kind of sign that you belonged to God's people and that His covenant blessings enfolded both you and your descendants forever. And so to lose your land and have your name disappear from the rolls of the people of God was a terrible prospect indeed. That has been the great crisis that the storyline has sought to resolve.

But Boaz stands in a position to rescue Naomi and Ruth and preserve the family name for good by marrying Ruth the Moabitess. However, there is someone else more closely related to Elimelech than he. There is a nearer kinsman redeemer and he has the prior claim, so that, whatever his own feelings in the matter, Boaz simply cannot redeem Ruth and Naomi unless the nearer redeemer refuses to do so.

And now, as we turn to the opening 12 verses of chapter 4 to see how things will go, we notice immediately that Ruth and Naomi temporarily disappear from the story. They almost drop out of view. In fact, there is no direct speech attributed to them in the remainder of the book of Ruth. From this point on, the spotlight falls almost entirely on Boaz. And as we watch him acting on behalf of Naomi and Ruth, we are being taught about the kind of Savior we need, the kind of service we owe, and the kind of salvation we receive.

1. The Kind of Savior We Need

Boaz is a man of his word. The night before, he had promised to act quickly, and now that the sun has risen it looks as though he has gone directly from the threshing floor to the city gate and sat down there (v. 1). The city gate in those days was the equivalent of city hall or perhaps the county courthouse. It was the place of business and judicial decision. By sitting down here, Boaz was giving public notice of his intention to conduct a legal transaction. And once again the narrator highlights the marvelous providence of God. Just as Boaz takes his seat in the gate, 'Behold, the redeemer of whom Boaz had spoken came by.' Impeccable timing. Here is God-the-Matchmaker at work. He paces Boaz' steps from the threshing floor to the city gate perfectly, doesn't He? Just as Boaz sits down, you would never guess who happened to be passing. The very man Boaz needs to see. It's a clue to us that however nervous Naomi, Ruth, or Boaz might be feeling at this moment in the story, *we* needn't be afraid. God has perfect timing, and He will work His purposes out for the good of His people and the glory of His name.

So Boaz seizes the bull by the horns: 'Turn aside, friend,' he says, 'and sit down here.' He quickly convenes the court, calling ten of the city elders to join them, and begins to present his case. Notice how he addresses the nearer redeemer: 'Naomi, who has come back from the country of Moab, is selling the parcel of land that belonged to our relative Elimelech. So I thought I would tell you of it and say, "Buy it in the presence of the elders of my people." If you will redeem it, redeem it. But if you will not, tell me, that I may know, for there is no one besides you to redeem it, and I come after you' (vv. 3-4). In other words, 'this looks like a wonderful business opportunity.' Naomi is selling, not actually the land itself, but the rights to the use and profits of the land – what's called the *usufruct* – in order to provide for herself and her daughter-in-law in their destitution. If the nearer redeemer would buy the field, he would ensure that it stayed within the same clan from which Elimelech had come. And, perhaps unsurprisingly, the man is immediately excited by the prospect of enlarging his portfolio. 'I will redeem it,' he says without any hesitation (v. 4).

But being the honors graduate of the internationally renowned Bethlehem School of Law and Agriculture that he was, Boaz very skillfully follows up with the second part of the bargain. 'You will redeem the land?' he says in effect in verses 5 and 6. 'Oh, that's great news. Naomi will be so relieved. Just sign here, and here, and here, and initial here, here, and here… and while you're doing that, there's one more thing… It's a small matter really. Your new real estate comes with a mother-in-law, a new wife, and the obligation to raise a son, on your own dime, of course, until he is old enough to take back the land on behalf of Ruth's dead husband and her father-in-law… So… as I was saying… if you'd just sign here and here….' It's a masterstroke of careful negotiation.

And as Boaz speaks, we watch, mid-transaction, as the blood drains from the face of the nearer redeemer. Suddenly he changes his tune. 'I cannot redeem it for myself,' he says, 'lest I impair my own inheritance' (v. 6). He was perfectly happy to help Naomi and Ruth out of a tight spot when it looked like he would gain a profitable parcel of land from the business deal. But it's another matter entirely now he knows that along with the land he would get all the responsibility for Elimelech's dependents. Any son that Ruth bore him would be considered *Elimelech's* heir, not his own, and the parcel of land he purchased that day would not belong to him in the end, but to the heir. And so now he's worried that Naomi and Ruth will bleed him dry. 'I would endanger my own inheritance while trying to save theirs. No, thank you.'

You see what's going on? While he stood to gain he was happy to be a redeemer, but not if it cost him too much. But Boaz isn't like that. And when the man tells Boaz to redeem it in his place, Boaz is quick to perform the strange little ritual that sealed the deal in verses 7-8. The nearer redeemer gave his sandal to Boaz. I suppose a close analogy would be like spitting in one's hand and shaking on a promise. He gave Boaz his sandal, and the contract was settled. Boaz called for the elders to bear witness. He has now bought the field, and much more than that. With a note of triumph, he declares that he has finally acquired Ruth to be his wife. *He* will be the one to preserve the name and allotment of Elimelech's family forever. Remember, however, that Boaz would have to bear the same cost and incur the same risks as the other redeemer. But, whereas he would not risk his own bankruptcy, *Boaz* is willing to commit everything to redeem Naomi and Ruth, and secure the name of the family of Elimelech. He acts unhesitatingly. He acts wisely. He acts faithfully, keeping his promise to Ruth and Naomi. And above all, he acts sacrificially. He willingly shoulders the obligation, even if in doing so it will be to his detriment. Isn't this the kind of Savior we need too? We need a redeemer who will save us at his own great cost. One who loves us and has given himself for us. Boaz is a picture to us of the Lord Jesus Christ.

To be sure, there are alternatives out there, other so-called redeemers who seem to promise much, and to whom we may at first turn. There is the whole array of empty religion. There are the countless outlets for the pursuit of mere pleasure that our culture says will set you free if you will only devote yourself to them. You can rest your hope for significance and satisfaction and rest in the family, in the intellect, or in some vague and ill-defined spirituality. They all seem – at first – to be effective redeemers, but none will do for us what the Greater-than-Boaz has already done. He is the one who, though He was rich, became poor for our sakes, so that we by His poverty might become rich (2 Cor. 8:9). He is the one who 'humbled himself by becoming obedient to the point of death, even death on a cross' (Phil. 2:8). The Lord Jesus Christ alone gives *Himself*, bears the price, and pays in full for the redemption of His people. As Paul puts it in Romans 3:23 and

24, though 'all have sinned and fall short of the glory of God'
we are 'justified freely by his grace through the redemption
that is in Christ Jesus' (NKJV). Jesus is our true redeemer. He
bears all the cost of our salvation. We have nothing to pay. He
incurs the full obligation. And pays it with His life-blood at
Calvary. Have you been wasting your time chasing the wrong
redeemer, one who will never save you in the end? It's Jesus
you need. It's Jesus you need.

2. The Service We Owe

When Boaz met the other redeemer at the gate that morning,
notice in verse 1 how he addresses him. 'Turn aside, friend,' he
says. 'Sit down here.' The phrase translated *friend* in our version
is the Hebrew expression 'ploni-almoni'. The New Jewish
Publication Society Version translates it as 'Mr. So and So'.[1]
The writer is highlighting his namelessness. He might simply
have referred to him as 'the man', or, 'the nearer redeemer'.
But the narrator actually resorts to calling him names. Mr. So
and So. He's telling us something important about him. And
we begin to grasp what it is when we remember that a central
concern of the book of Ruth is for the preservation of *the name*
of Elimelech.

The great irony of this part of the story is that the man who
is in first place to secure the preservation of Elimelech's family
name is the one man whose name is deliberately hidden and
obscured by the narrator. He is just *Mr. So and So*. His name is
forgotten. It is blotted out of the record. We don't know who he
is. Throughout the Bible having your name blotted out is a terrible prospect. It is symbolic of the curse and condemnation of
God. So for example, in Deuteronomy 9:14, in His wrath, God
threatened to 'blot out the name' of Israel from under heaven.
Or in Psalm 109:13 there is a curse on the wicked that echoes
much of the message of the book of Ruth; 'May his posterity
be cut off,' the psalmist prays. 'May his name be blotted out in
the second generation.' That is what *Mr. So and So* could have
avoided for Elimelech, but that is precisely what he ended up
experiencing for himself. His name was blotted out.

---

1. Jewish Publication Society, *Tanakh*, *NJPSV* (Nebraska: University of
Nebraska Press: 1985), p. 1423.

There are two redeemers in the passage. One serves only himself – and has no name. Boaz, on the other hand, serves others selflessly and his name has never been blotted out. You will recall that the Lord Jesus said, 'Whoever loves his life loses it, and whoever hates his life in this world will keep it for eternal life. If anyone serves me, he must follow me; and where I am, there will my servant be also. If anyone serves me, the Father will honor him' (John 12:25-26). Isn't that precisely the message here? Whoever loves his life loses it, and whoever hates his life in this world will keep it for eternal life. Whoever seeks to make a name for themselves at the expense of others loses their name in the end. But whoever is willing to give all to redeem others, their names are never forgotten. Think of those names on the memorial in Postman's Park in London. Their selfless sacrifices on behalf of others has preserved the memory of their names. That was Boaz. That is the Christian life. That is our calling if we are followers of Jesus Christ. To be sure, Boaz reminds us of Jesus in his selfless sacrificial service. But the question we must face is whether our lives would do the same? Will your name be preserved in the book of life or will you be just another Mr. or Mrs. So and So, who, despite their words, lived a life that showed they did not know or follow the Lord Jesus Christ?

3. The Salvation We Receive

Notice the blessing of the elders pronounced on Boaz and Ruth, as their future marriage is secured in verses 11 and 12: 'We are witnesses. May the LORD make the woman, who is coming into your house, like Rachel and Leah, who together built up the house of Israel. May you act worthily in Ephrathah and be renowned in Bethlehem, and may your house be like the house of Perez, whom Tamar bore to Judah, because of the offspring that the LORD will give you by this young woman.'

Leah and Rachel were the wives of Israel's patriarch, Jacob. By comparing Ruth to Rachel and Leah these elders are saying something incredibly significant about this Moabitess. The same thing is true of their prayer that Ruth's son would be like Perez whom Tamar bore Judah in Genesis 38. Judah was Boaz's direct ancestor, and Bethlehem Ephrathah belonged to the territory allotted to the tribe of Judah. Tamar, like Ruth, was a Gentile. Tamar, like Ruth, bore Perez through levirate marriage. Though unlike Ruth, Tamar's actions were seedy and manipulative, whereas Ruth acted with godly purity and integrity.

In making those connections they were recognizing Ruth as a true Israelite even though she was a Moabite by birth. They were saying that she *belongs* as much as, and they were praying that she would have a role *analogous to,* Rachel and Leah and Tamar. It's almost as if they had some sense that this marriage portends great future blessing, not just for Boaz and Ruth, but for the whole people of God. And so it will, as we will see when studying the next section of the book. For now, let us grasp clearly that Ruth the outsider is now Ruth the insider. Ruth the stranger, Ruth the Moabitess, is now Ruth the heir of Israel's matriarchs and the caretaker of Judah's future. That is what the kinsman redeemer Boaz does for her.

That is really what Jesus Christ does for His people. He takes them from outside and brings them inside. He takes them from a place of exclusion and alienation and brings them into the family of God. 'Remember that at one time you Gentiles in the flesh... were... separated from Christ, alienated from the commonwealth of Israel and strangers to the covenants of promise, having no hope and without God in the world. But now in Christ Jesus, you who once were far off have been brought near by the blood of Christ... So then you are no longer strangers and aliens, but you are fellow citizens with the saints and members of the household of God,' as Paul put it in Ephesians 2:11-19.

When you come to trust our true Kinsman-Redeemer, the Lord Jesus Christ, you stop being a stranger to the people of God and become a member of the family. No matter how far outside you may think yourself, through Jesus Christ there is a way into the family and household of God. The gospel makes insiders of those outside. The gospel brings Moabites and makes them heirs of the rich heritage of the people of God. The gospel makes of sinners, saints. It forgives the guilty, cleanses the dirty, releases the captives, and sets the prisoners free. There is room for you. There is room for you. You are invited in. All you need is a Kinsman-Redeemer.

As we have already noted, one of the remarkable features of the fourth chapter of the book of Ruth is that all the action is driven along, for the first time in the story, not by Naomi, not by Ruth, but by Boaz. The opening sentence of chapter 4 features an unusual sentence structure in Hebrew, placing the subject before the verb. Boaz is the first word. Boaz is highlighted. Our eyes fall on Boaz. And as you scan through the chapter, almost all the active verbs relate to Boaz. Boaz is the actor on behalf of Ruth and Naomi. They are passive. Their stance is summed up in the last verse of chapter 3: 'Wait my daughter,' Naomi tells Ruth, 'until you learn how the matter turns out, for the man, Boaz, will not rest but will settle the matter today.' How do you come in from outside, right into the family and household of God? You do it by no work of your own. You do it by resting, like Naomi and Ruth, entirely on the work of your Kinsman-Redeemer, the Lord Jesus Christ. He has done everything necessary to save you. There is nothing for you to do, but trust Him; nothing to do but wait, confident that He will settle the matter. 'He is the propitiation for our sins,' 1 John 2:2 says, 'and not for ours only, but for the whole world.' There is room for you in the kingdom of God because Jesus has done it all – paid in full at the cross – and the whole world full of lost and helpless sinners is invited to come to Him for rest.

Do you have a kinsman redeemer, in Jesus? He alone can give you a name written indelibly in the book of life. Without Him, like *Mr So and So* in our text, your name will be blotted out forever. Take Naomi and Ruth's stance. Wait, trusting the greater than Boaz to act for you. He did not rest until He had settled the matter, having died for sinners just like you. There is no-one so far away, no-one so lost, that through faith alone in Jesus Christ, you, who once were strangers and aliens, without hope and without God in the world, cannot be brought near and made fellow citizens and members of the household of God. May the Lord help us look to Christ, a perfect Redeemer.

6

The Meaning of Marriage
(Ruth 4:13-21)

It has become fashionable today in movie scripts for there to be no happy ending. The romantic comedy where boy meets girl, they fall for one another, then they break up, and then... Well, it used to be that the movie would end with the relationship being restored, and they'd live happily ever after. But nowadays, they break up and the movie just ends. I *hate* that. Don't you feel cheated? It's like a sneeze that never quite happens. There's this big build up and then... nothing. Of course, it may just be because we've wasted two perfectly good hours watching a story that goes nowhere, but I think there's a deeper reason we find stories like that so unsatisfying. I think it's because we are hard-wired for redemption. We want stories with complete narrative arcs that move from crisis to complete resolution. It may not be cool or edgy or postmodern, but we still love a happy ending, don't we? We want stories with complete redemptive arcs.

Of course, that's one of the reasons the book of Ruth is so compelling. It doesn't leave us hanging. There is a complete resolution to the crisis introduced at the beginning of the story. Actually, as we'll see, the resolution to this story transcends our expectations in wonderful ways. People sometimes argue that the difference between myth and fact is that in myth the boundaries of what is possible are removed and the redemptive resolution to a story can be fantastical and imaginative and surprising. But the *real* difference between myth and fact is that the redemptive resolution of a make-believe story is always limited by the imagination of the author, however fantastical it may be. But in a factual account of real divine redemption breaking into human experience, like the account before us in the book of Ruth, the redemptive resolution always exceeds our wildest imaginings. It is altogether *more* wonderful. And with that in mind, we turn now to the last section of the book of Ruth as the final resolution of the drama takes place. And as we watch all the loose ends in the story finally being tied off, we are actually being taught about the nature of the salvation God provides.

1. Salvation is Not a Transaction. It's a Marriage.

'So Boaz took Ruth, and she became his wife. And he went into her, and the LORD gave her conception, and she bore a son' (v. 13). The language there – 'Boaz took Ruth' – highlights an aspect of the marriage ritual in those days, according to Deuteronomy 20:7. The bridegroom brought his bride into his own home. Boaz took Ruth into his house. The elders referred to that part of the marriage custom back in verse 11: 'May the LORD make the woman who is coming into your house like Rachel.' Boaz has publicly secured the legal right to marry Ruth, and by taking her into his own home he has completed their union.

It's interesting to notice that as the storyline has progressed towards this climactic moment, Ruth has gone on a journey too. It's not just a geographical journey from Moab to Bethlehem, but a journey from one status to another. In 2:10, she referred to herself as a 'foreigner' and in 2:13 as a 'servant' or even a 'slave'. In 3:9, she is a 'maidservant'. But now in 4:13, she has become a 'wife'. Ruth has been utterly transformed – from an outsider and a foreigner to a slave, to a maidservant, to a wife. This Moabite girl is likened, in the blessing of the elders in verses 11 and 12, to the matriarchs of Israel. Everything about Ruth has been changed forever. And it's vital that we understand how that has happened. How has her story been reversed so completely? Her story has been reversed because Boaz has married her. And while the levirate laws and the customs of ancient Israel no longer obtain today, while we no longer have kinsmen redeemers, we still understand something of Ruth's experience.

The fact is, there are very few things more life-altering than marriage. When a man and a woman are joined in marriage, they cease to be what they were. The two become one flesh, the Bible says (Gen. 2:4; Matt. 19:5,6). It is a union that is utterly transformative. Those of us who are married are bound to confess that we are who we are in no small measure because of the profound bond we share with our spouses, which is why the Bible uses marriage as a key metaphor to describe the union of God with Israel, and Christ with His Church. As Paul puts it in Ephesians 5:25-32:

> Husbands, love your wives, as Christ loved the church and gave himself up for her, that he might sanctify her, having cleansed her by the washing of water with the word, so that he might present the church to himself in splendor, without spot or wrinkle or any such thing, that she might be holy and without blemish… 'Therefore, a man shall leave his father and mother and hold fast to his wife, and the two shall become one flesh.' This mystery is profound, and I am saying that it refers to Christ and the church.

Throughout the story of Ruth, we have found in Boaz a picture of the perfect redeemer to come, the Lord Jesus Christ. Here we learn how it is that our redeemer, Jesus, takes us from being unwelcome outsiders, like Ruth the Moabitess, and brings us to belong in the central stream of the life of God's people. He does it by taking a foreigner and making her His bride. Christ saves His church by loving her and giving Himself up for her to sanctify and cleanse her, and make her splendid and radiant, holy and without blemish. That is how Christ has loved you. Not from a distance. But as a bridegroom who gives himself for his bride.

When we read, back in verses 1-11, of the formal transaction Boaz conducted at the gate of the city as he secured the rights to marry Ruth, it might have seemed at first like a cold, legal business – hardly the most romantic preparations for a marriage. And it may at times be tempting to think of the Christian gospel in similar terms: as a desiccated and dry abstraction; a cold, legal business; a thing of doctrines and duties and nothing more. But the truth is, if you are a Christian, you have been redeemed because you have been beloved by the Bridegroom Himself, who has pursued you and made you His own. You are a Christian because Jesus Christ has given His life to redeem you for Himself. 'From heaven he came and sought her to be his holy bride, with his own blood he bought her, and for her life he died.'[1] That's how Jesus loves the church.

But, as we trace the rather satisfying and complete redemptive narrative arc in the book of Ruth, the truth is we may yet feel that the narrative arc of our own storyline remains unresolved, unsatisfying, or incomplete. But if we have the Greater-than-Boaz for our redeemer, we can have perfect confidence that one day soon our Bridegroom Himself will come to take us into His house, and make all things new. 'Then I saw a new heaven and a new earth,' the apostle John writes, and he goes on, 'I saw the holy city, New Jerusalem, coming down out of heaven from God, prepared as a bride adorned for her husband. And I heard a loud voice from the throne saying, "Behold, the dwelling of God is with man, he will dwell with them, and they will be his people, and God himself will be with them as their God. He will wipe away every tear from their eyes, and death shall be no more, neither shall there be mourning, nor crying nor pain anymore, for the former things have passed away"' (Rev. 21:1-4). That is the promise of our Bridegroom.

The complete redemptive arc of Ruth's storyline is a small-scale echo of the complete redemptive arc of the biblical storyline as a whole. And that means that the very same redemptive arc will find its perfect mirror in the storyline of your life too one day soon, if you are a believer in the Lord Jesus Christ. Salvation is no mere transaction, after all. It's a *marriage*. We are united to Christ, as to a bridegroom.

2. Salvation is Not an Idea. It's Personal.
Look at verse 13, again. It compresses nine whole months into a single sentence. Boaz and Ruth get pregnant right away. It sometimes happens that way, doesn't it? But remember

---

1. From S. J. Stone's 1866 hymn, *The Church's One Foundation*.

what that means within the story of the book of Ruth. What is the great crisis that only Boaz can resolve? The crisis is that with Elimelech's death, and the death of his two sons, Mahlon and Chilion, Elimelech's family name and allotment in the Land of Promise will surely be lost and Naomi and Ruth will be destitute and alone forever. But that means that to have a son by Boaz was an event of enormous significance. Elimelech now has an heir. His line will continue. There is hope and a future.

Actually, the narrator underscores just how important the birth of this child really is in at least four ways. First of all, notice the language of verse 13 carefully: 'The LORD gave her conception, and she bore a son.' That is a hugely important statement. The only other time the LORD is the subject of a verb in the book of Ruth is back at the very beginning of the story, in 1:6. Just at the point when Naomi and Ruth resolve to return after ten long, disastrous years in the land of Moab we are told that 'the LORD visited his people and gave them food'. And now here, at the other end of the story, a similar construction is used again. The LORD is visiting His people again, not to give them food this time, but to give them a child. It's a beautiful way to underscore that this baby is not like any other born in Israel in those days. This baby was a child of promise, a child of destiny. His arrival was the result of a divine visitation.

Then secondly, the writer underscores the importance of this child by using a Hebrew expression that occurs in only two other places in all of scripture, most significantly in Genesis 3:16 to describe the curse of God on Eve who will conceive and bear children in pain, yet whose son would nevertheless one day crush the serpent's head. Ruth is like a new Eve, whose child bears the weight of the covenant promise of God.

Then thirdly, remember that Ruth, though she had previously been married to Mahlon for ten years, nevertheless had no children. But now 'the LORD gave her conception', and with those words she enters the rolls of those women of the Bible to whom God gave sons when, humanly speaking, having children seemed quite impossible. So Ruth the Moabitess takes her place along with Sarah, and Hannah, and Elizabeth, and especially, alongside Mary, the mother of Jesus, as the mother of a child of destiny.

And finally, in verse 17, you will see the name the women of Bethlehem give to Ruth and Boaz's baby boy, 'They named him Obed.' Wonderfully, Obed means 'servant'. Now put it all together. Do you see what we are being taught? Here is a child whose coming is the result of divine visitation, whose conception portrays Ruth as a new Eve, and places Ruth among the mothers of Israel's heroes, and his name is Servant. If Boaz is a picture of Christ as he marries Ruth, so too, very clearly, is his son, in whom the hope of Ruth's redemption is fully realized. Obed directs our attention away from himself to Jesus. *Jesus* is the baby of Bethlehem in whom God has visited the world. *Jesus* is Eve's son who crushes the serpent's head. *Jesus* is the Son of the virgin to whom 'the Lord gave conception'. And, as Isaiah 53, makes plain, *Jesus* is the Servant, upon whom the Lord has laid the iniquities of us all, and by whose stripes we are healed. It's impossible not to be thinking of Christ if you read this part of Ruth with care.

But just in case you somehow missed the signposts to Jesus thus far, the narrator drops all pretense of subtlety, he stops playing a finesse game, and picks up a sledgehammer and pounds home the hope of a King to save Israel with unmistakable clarity in verses 17-22: 'Obed was the father of Jesse, the father of David. Now these are the generations of Perez: Perez fathered Hezron, Hezron fathered Ram, Ram fathered Amminadab, Amminadab fathered Nahshon, Nahshon fathered Salmon, Salmon fathered Boaz, Boaz fathered Obed, Obed fathered Jesse, and Jesse fathered David.'

What was God doing in the story of the book of Ruth? He was certainly taking a Moabitess and making her a child of God. That's true. But he was doing much, much more. He was at work to secure the birth of Obed, the Servant, whose arrival ensured the preservation of the line from which David would come, Israel's great King. He in turn would be the one from whom the Son of David, the King of the Jews, the Savior of the World, the Lord Jesus Christ would descend. What is the book of Ruth really? Isn't it the gospel of Jesus Christ, the Servant King, who makes outsiders His Bride and redeems them by means of the Cross? The genealogy here is designed to rivet our gaze upon the child of the child of the child of the union between Boaz and Ruth who would be the final Servant, the Savior of the world.

I read recently a moving missionary story that highlights wonderfully how the genealogy with which Ruth concludes should function for us. Des and Jenny Oatridge were Bible translators working among the remote Binumarien tribe in Papua New Guinea. They spent ten years living and working among them, witnessing for Christ, and reducing the Binumarien language to writing and producing portions of the scriptures in their native tongue. But in all those years they had very little success in winning anyone to faith in Jesus. One day that all changed. They just finished translating the gospel of Matthew, but they had forgotten to translate the first seventeen verses. They worked with a native man called Sisia who assisted them in the translation work. To their surprise Sisia sailed through the passage, translating it with eagerness and without any hint of boredom. When he was finished, he stood and declared, 'There's going to be an important meeting in Nameepi's house tonight. I want you to come and bring what we've done today.'

When Des arrived later that night Nameepi's house was packed and overflowing. There was an odd sense of tension in the air that made him nervous. He was led to a seat on the floor beside the fire in the middle of the room. Then Sisia immediately spoke up. 'I have asked Mata'a Des to come and read what we translated this morning. I can't tell it to you. I want you to hear it for yourselves.' The room became extraordinarily still. Des was conscious that all eyes were focused on him. He cleared his throat and began to read: 'These are the ancestors of Jesus Messiah, a descendant of King David and of Abraham. Abraham was the father of Isaac; Isaac was the father of Jacob; Jacob was the father of Judah and his brothers; Judah was the father of Perez and Zerah.'

Des could not look up. His eyes were glued to the text. He was trying to read as naturally as Sisia had spoken the sentences to him that morning, but the tense atmosphere in the room made this difficult. He did not see Fofondai's eyes grow wider and rounder, as did Maraa'aro's and several others near him. He could sense, though, that every word he spoke was being grabbed and critically examined by the listeners. He became conscious that Yawo was moving near to him. So were A'aaso, Aaka and Yaa'a. He was aware Sao watched his lips unblinkingly. As he continued reading, more and more people began pressing. The people from the other rooms were pushing into the central room. Fofo was so close that his beard almost touched the written page. Yawo's arm was rammed right against Des'. Des suddenly felt scared. He had a sense of being crushed. It was not only the pressure of bodies; it was the uncanny silence. It seemed that not a dog barked, not a baby cried, not a person released his breath.

He did not know if the list of names offended some ritual taboo about which he knew nothing. If so, and the people were angry that it was being so blatantly publicized, he was in an awkward position. There was no way of escape, hemmed in as he was. And with the atmosphere so charged, he felt he dared not ask a question. These people were so volatile; they could erupt in a fury so easily. So he kept on reading. 'Matthan was the father of Jacob; Jacob was the father of Joseph (who was the husband of Mary, the mother of Jesus the Messiah). There are fourteen generations from Abraham to King David; and fourteen from King David's time until the exile in Babylon; and fourteen from the exile to Christ.'

They had heard him out. Des raised his eyes to look at those within a breath of his face and saw, not anger, but incredulity. 'Why didn't you tell us all this before?' Yaa'a demanded. Des recoiled instinctively as if he'd been struck. 'No-one bothers to write down the ancestors of spirit beings,' Fofondai stated. 'It's only real people who record their genealogical table,' A'aaso added. 'Jesus must be a real person.' someone else cried, his voice ringing with astonishment. Then everyone seemed to be talking at once. 'Fourteen generations, that's two hands and a foot, from Abraham to King David. Two more hands and a foot, to the time of the calibus, the captivity, and another two hands and a foot till Jesus' time.' 'That's a very, very long time. This ancestry goes back further than ours. Yes, none of ours goes back two hands and a foot three times.' 'Jesus must have been a real man on this earth then. He's not just white man's magic.' 'Then what the mission has taught us is real.'

Yes, real. Des pondered on that as he made his way home. The ancient list of names which he had always found boring and pretty well meaningless had ratified Jesus as a real person to his unlettered friends. He possessed a genealogy like their own. To the Binumariens, the truth of the scriptures was now beyond doubt.[2]

God was at work when He sent Naomi to Moab with Elimelech. And He was at work when He brought Naomi and Ruth back, broken and bereft and alone in the grief and bitterness. He was at work when He brought Ruth into the field of Boaz that day, and at work when Boaz met the other redeemer at the city gate. He was at work when Boaz and Ruth married and conceived Obed. And He was at work when Obed fathered Jesse, and Jesse fathered David. In it all, God was at work to give you Jesus, great David's greater Son. The genealogy of Jesus Christ – the first part of which is being written here at the end of the book of Ruth – the genealogy of Jesus Christ functions like the landing lights that illuminate the runway at night for planes coming into the airport. It guides us, generation by generation, towards the only safe place to land in the darkness. It directs us safely to Christ. Salvation is not a mere transaction; it's a marriage, a union. But neither is it mere data, a mere idea, a worldview or concept. It is profoundly personal. To know the saving grace of God is to know Jesus Christ, 'This is eternal life,' Jesus said, "that you may know God and Jesus whom he has sent' (John 17:3). Whatever your level of knowledge, however committed to living morally, however religiously observant you may be, the great pressing question the book of Ruth demands that we all answer is this – Do you know Jesus Christ? Do you know Him? He is real. And salvation is found in fellowship, in connection with Him.

3. Salvation is not superficial. Its comprehensive.

Notice how the women of the town pronounce their blessing upon Naomi: 'The LORD has not left her without a redeemer, whose name would be famous in Israel. He will restore her life and nourish her in old age' (vv. 14-15). Her redeemer is

---

2. Oates, Lynette. 'How the Binumarien people of New Guinea discovered Jesus is real.' Creation.com. October 09, 2012. Accessed August 9, 2016. http://www.wycliffe.org.au/shop/.

the child born to Ruth. The baby Boaz and Ruth produce is the catalyst for the final and complete reversal of Naomi's brokenness and is the certain provider of Naomi's future. What will this union with Christ, that's likened in scripture to a marriage, accomplish? What is it that that knowing Jesus personally will do for you? Look at the passage; Obed, the servant, will redeem Naomi by restoring her life and nourishing her in her old age.

What a delightful picture of the complete reversal of Naomi's fortunes. You remember the outline of her story? She went away from Bethlehem, with her husband Elimelech and her two sons, Mahlon, and Chilion in tow. She 'went away full,' she said. But after ten catastrophic years in Moab, where Elimelech and their two boys all perished, she 'came back empty.' 'Do not call me Naomi' – pleasant – 'but call me Mara – bitter. For the LORD has dealt very bitterly with me.' And we've watched as God directed Ruth's and Boaz' lives towards one another, and all the time He was pursuing Naomi's heart, wooing her back to Him. We've seen hope rekindle within her. We've seen her take miss-steps and wrong turns along the way. And we've seen her come, at the end of chapter 3, to a place of total trust in the work of another, in the work of a redeemer, in Boaz instead of her own efforts. And now, as the book comes to a conclusion, we see God lavishing full restoration upon her: 'He will restore your life and nourish you in your old age' (v. 15).

Isn't that what Jesus gives us? 'I have come that you may have life,' Jesus said, 'and life in abundance' (John 10:10). Jesus is the restorer of our lives and the nourisher of our years. He is the fountain of living water. The vine, in union with whom the branches all have their life, apart from whom we can do nothing. The salvation Jesus gives is not some superficial, surface change. It's not an addition to your life as it now is. No, it is new life, renewed life, renovated life. And it's available to you only in Him. We've watched God-the-Matchmaker leading Ruth into the arms of Boaz, and we watched Him lead Naomi back to Himself. But the final purpose of God in the book of Ruth is to lead you into the arms of Jesus, to bring you to your Bridegroom, and to make you say, 'I am my beloved's and he is mine. Christ is all in all to me. Fairer than ten thousand.' Do you have Christ? Do you know Christ? Is your Christianity an idea, an abstraction, a moral code? If it is, it is an empty shell and a worthless imitation. It is Christ to whom the book of Ruth points us. He is all in all, and all you could ever need; the restorer of your lives and the nourisher of your years. May the Lord bring us to Him.

Bibliography

Block, Daniel I., *Judges, Ruth* (Nashville, TN: Broadman and Holman, 1999).

Duguid, Iain M., *Esther and Ruth* (Phillipsburg, NJ: P & R Publishing, 2005).

Jewish Publication Society, *Tanakh, NJPSV* (Nebraska: University of Nebraska Press: 1985).

Matthews, Victor H., *Judges and Ruth* (New York, NY: Cambridge University Press, 2004).

Mead, Rev. Matthew, *The Almost Christian Discovered: Or, the False Professor Tried and Cast* (CreateSpace Independent Publishing Platform, 2013).

Oates, Lynette, 'How the Binumarien people of New Guinea discovered Jesus is real.' (Creation.com. October 09, 2012. Accessed August 9, 2016. http://www.wycliffe.org.au/shop/).

Trinity Hymnal (Philadelphia: Great Commission Publications,1990).

Watson, Thomas, *The Godly Man's Picture* (Edinburgh, UK: Banner of Truth, 1992).

Esther
Sudden Reversals

I

The Lord Reigns
(Esther 1:1-22)

What do you do when it seems like God is not there? How are we to make sense of things when our convictions about God and His goodness and love for us seem to be contradicted by our lives and experience, or when you seek to be faithful to Him and He seems to be nowhere to be found? The Book of Esther is one place where the Bible itself asks and answers those questions. As some of us have discovered after many bitter tears, the fact that the Bible does not shrink from such questions is almost as helpful to us when we find ourselves wrestling with them as the answers it provides. Our faith is not shaken simply by asking hard questions; rather, our faith is shaken when we ask them laboring under the mistaken impression that somehow the Word of God does not anticipate questions like that, or that it does not itself ask such questions, or that it cannot speak to them with real world honesty.

You may have noticed in reading the opening chapter of Esther the conspicuous absence of the name of God, or of any mention of the supernatural, or of prayer, or worship. In fact, if you scan through Esther you will see that that is true of the book as a whole. God seems, at first glance at least, to be entirely absent from the story. Which, let's be honest, is sometimes just how we feel about our own circumstances. Everything is going wrong. Where is God? And yet, the key idea the book of Esther wants to help us begin to see, is that *the presence of absence is not the same as the absence of presence*. Just because God is not listed in the *dramatis personae* along with Esther and Mordecai, Ahasueras and Haman, we would miss the message of the book entirely if we did not realize that, however important these characters are, Almighty God Himself is the principal actor in the whole drama. God does not appear in various contexts, showing up here and there, playing bit parts, like an extra in the play of our lives. No, the point the book of Esther makes is that the life pattern of each of the human players in the story, and ultimately of our own lives too, is lived out in the larger context of God's ceaseless and sovereign activity. He is no extra in the drama of our lives. But we are all players in a drama of which He is the author and the director and the principle character.

And so as we turn to the opening chapter of the book, we need to keep in mind that principle: *The presence of absence is not the same as the absence of presence*. God is not named in these chapters. But His hand is everywhere. God does not speak in these chapters, but the characteristic signs of the direction of providence are all over our text, communicating as loudly as any prophetic oracle how we are to understand the events as they unfold.

The scene opens in the banqueting chambers of King Ahasueras at Susa. In fact, the whole book is bracketed by two banquets. It opens with a feast here in Chapter 1, and it closes with a feast in chapters 9 and 10. Part of the agenda of the book of Esther is to move us from one kind of feast – held for one set of reasons – to another kind of feast entirely: from the counterfeit to the real, from the empty to the substantial, from the fading joys of the worldling to 'the solid joys and lasting pleasures none but Zion's children know'.[1]

1. The Satire: How the King Displays His Own Glory
In this case the author of the book leaves us in no doubt at all about the kind of feast with which the story begins. The whole thing is carefully staged by Ahasueras to display his own

---

1. From the fourth stanza of the well-known hymn, 'Glorious Things of Thee Are Spoken.'

glory, and our author goes out of his way to drive that home to us. First, we learn about the virtually limitless power of this man (1:1-3). He rules a vast empire, we are told, from India to Ethiopia: 127 provinces. He's the supreme ruler of *the* world superpower of the day. Then, secondly, we learn about the vast possessions of this man. Look at verses 4-8. He shows his lieutenants 'the riches of his royal glory and the splendor and pomp of his greatness for many days, 180 days.' And when this feast was over a second festival began, this time for the common citizenry of the city, lasting another week. And look at verse 6. The Hebrew is unusual there. One commentator tries to capture the sense of it by translating verse 6, 'And Oh! The white cotton curtains and violet hangings … and oh! The couches of gold and silver on a mosaic pavement of porphyry marble, mother of pearl and precious stones.'[2] Oh, the grandeur. Oh, the glory! Oh, the opulence! This was a palace designed to stun, to take your breath away, and to leave you in no doubt about the wealth of the king.

Verses 7 and 8 tell us the wine was flowing freely. In verse 8 Ahasueras declares the drinking rule, 'There is no compulsion.' Now there is an irony there. As one writer remarks, 'In an autocracy *even the absence of a rule requires a decree.*'[3] It is hard not to smirk a little at the micromanaging megalomania of the king that needs to legislate for how people drink at his parties, which, by the way, is exactly what the author of the book is aiming at. Ahasueras *wants* us to bow before him in awe and reverence. He *wants* to be adored by his subjects and feared by his enemies and obeyed by everyone. He *wants* total control.

2. The Irony: How Empty and Limited the King's Power Really Is

But as the next scene unfolds, the author of Esther is unflinching in exposing how empty and limited the king's power really is. As the party reaches its climax, and Ahasueras is full of

---

2. Frederic Bush, *Ruth/Esther, Word Biblical Commentary* (Nashville, TN: Thomas Nelson, 1996), pp. 339, 347.

3. David G. Firth, *The Message of Esther* (Downers Grove, IL: InterVarsity Press 2010), p. 40.

wine, he summons his beautiful wife, Queen Vashti. He sends seven eunuchs to collect her. She is to come wearing her royal crown. And all 'in order,' note verse 11, 'to show the peoples and the princes her beauty, for she was lovely to look at.' You see how the king views his wife? He is not devoted to her, loving her, giving himself up for her in servant leadership.[4] To Ahasueras, Vashti is just another possession; literally a trophy wife. And he wants to show her off to make himself look good. Ahasueras has everything: near total power, unending riches, and a wife whose beauty is the crowning monument to his own towering ego. She is his tool, his plaything, and he wants to show her off before the leering stares of his generals.

But Vashti won't come. We don't know why. A great deal of ink has been spilled trying to supply a motive for Vashti's refusal. Was she a proto feminist? Was she more noble than the king? Is Vashti the heroine of the story? All of that is entirely beside the point. We really don't know anything about Vashti. Vashti is not the focus. The point, rather, is that suddenly, and very publicly indeed, Ahasueras' power, and might, and influence, and prestige and resources and money, are revealed as the empty things that they really are. With one lash of his pen, the author of the book of Esther paints Ahasueras for a fool. He has given himself to the pursuit of glory, but the most basic realities of life elude him. His marriage is a sham. His power is not total after all; his sovereignty is not absolute. His wife shrugs off the command of mighty Ahasueras. And everyone sees it.

And now, look at verse 12: 'But Queen Vashti refused to come at the king's command delivered by the eunuchs. At this the king became enraged, and his anger burned within him.' Ahasueras, the god-king, ruler of 127 provinces, from India to Ethiopia, is overcome by a temper tantrum. 'He that had rule over 127 provinces,' says Matthew Henry, 'had no rule over his own spirit.'[5] He was enraged. He who controlled the drinking habits of his subjects by royal decree could not

---

4. See Paul's description of the role of a husband in Ephesians 5:25-28.

5. Matthew Henry, *Commentary on the Whole Bible, Vol. II.* (New York: Revell, 1983), p. 1124.

so much as control his own temper. He summons his wise
men and they decide, in verses 13-22, that Vashti has got
to go. 'What a terrible example she is setting for the noble
women of Persia.' they say (v. 18). So she is never again to be
admitted to the king's presence. And more than that, it now
becomes universal law that, verse 22, 'every man be master
in his own household, and speak according to the language
of his people.' So now, all the power of the empire, with this
vast bureaucracy, will line up behind a royal command, given
in a moment of drunken anger, mandating that men should
be masters in their own homes. Do you see how laughable
that is? If we were to uncover the original manuscripts of
Esther I think we'd find a number of places where the writing
was erratic and shaky, because the author was laughing so
hard at the absurdity of human power flexing its muscles
and posturing at problems it cannot fix. Ahasueras is tilting
at windmills. He is trying to command the tide to turn. He's
making laws that cannot be enforced, so that each line of his
decree, written in a fit of pique, rather than underscoring his
greatness, serves only to unmask the vanity and impotence
and insecurity of this man and his values.

(i) Viewing the World from a New Perspective
And that brings us to the first thing we need to learn here.
In Esther chapter 1, we are being invited to *view the world
and its values from a new perspective*. The book of Esther wants
us to stop being dazzled by the trappings of earthly glory,
by wealth and prestige and power. In fact, it wants us to
recognize that not only is a life lived in pursuit of such things
empty and foolish, it is ultimately *laughable*. We are meant to
laugh at Ahasueras as a way to teach us to laugh at ourselves
and all the temptations of a world that fixates on what you
have, what you wear, what you do, who you know, where
you went to school. The author of Esther is laughing at the
ridiculous spectacle of Ahasueras, who does not realize that
'a man's life does not consist in the abundance of things'
(Luke 12:15), in the hope that that realization will begin to
dawn on us too.

But if Ahasueras appears ridiculous, '[h]ow much more
ridiculous are we…,' asks Iain Duguid, 'when we spend so

much time and energy desiring a new sports car, or a great pair of shoes at the mall, or the latest home improvement in the mail-order catalog? Ultimately, it's all empty. The emperor's costly clothes are transparent, and what may be seen through them by the discerning eye is ridiculous. True value lies in the values of an altogether different empire.'[6] Esther wants us to view the world and its values from a new perspective.

(ii) Viewing God's Providence with Renewed Patience
Then, secondly, in this opening chapter of Esther we are being taught *to view God's providence with renewed patience.* We are being taught the principle articulated by the Puritan John Flavel. 'Providence,' he said, 'is like a Hebrew word. It is best read backwards.' Esther 1 doesn't read like theology at all, does it? It is an entirely secular setting. It shows us pagan lives lived in the pursuit of earthly glory, oblivious to the Lord and unconcerned for His kingdom. His name is not mentioned and His purposes are unclear. But to rush to conclude that that must therefore mean that God is not involved, that all of this unfolds away from His gaze, would be a serious mistake. Just because we cannot see what God is doing or where He is to be found in our circumstances, just because we are not in a position to discern His design or plot the course He is taking, does not mean we should dismiss the presence and sovereignty of God out of hand. In fact, the drunken parties at Susa, the refusal of Vashti to become the object of lecherous stares, the temper tantrum of a spoiled king, the sycophantic flattery of his royal advisors, each play a vital role in opening the door for a young unknown Jewish peasant girl called Esther to rise to the throne and become the instrument of God's deliverance of His people.

Let's not be so quick to dismiss the mundane, even the dark and worldly details, as if God were not sovereign over them all. God is working, even in the avarice and greed and lust and pride of Ahasueras, for the glory of His name and the salvation of His people. Esther 1 aims to help us learn to take the long view, to wait and read the providence of God

---

6. Iain Duguid, *Esther and Ruth* (Phillipsburg, NJ: P&R Publishing, 2005), p. 14.

with hindsight, with the benefit of knowing – at last – what God was doing in those long dark days when you could not see His hand, nor discern His design. Esther 1 is a lesson in trust, asking us, 'Will you rest in the goodness of God even in the darkest of days when His purposes are obscured and unclear?'

(iii) Longing for A Different Kingdom and a Better King
And finally, Esther chapter 1 is intended to *make us long for a different kingdom and a better king.* Here is earthly power at its pinnacle. Here is the highest a person can rise in this world's estimation. Here is glory and influence and pleasure and success. But it leaves us with a bitter taste in our mouths as we read it. It leaves us uneasy, discontent, and struck again by the absurdity of a life lived for such things. It leaves us longing for a better kingdom and a better king; One whose rule is just, rather than capricious, One whose invitations to us are marked by love – not lust or a will to power. One who does not view his bride as an instrument for self- aggrandizement but who gives himself up for her. It leaves us longing for Jesus. His kingdom is not marked by external glory. He is unimpressed with the trappings of earthly influence and prestige. He does not choose many who are wise according to this world's standards, nor many who are powerful, nor many who are of noble birth, as Paul puts it in 1 Corinthians 1:26. That is not what Christ's kingdom looks like. No, he chooses the foolish and the weak and the low and despised in the world, even those that are not, to bring to nothing those that are, so that no human being might boast in the presence of God (1 Cor. 1:29).

Unlike Ahasueras, Jesus is a king who came not to be served but to serve, and to give His life a ransom for many. He is a king crowned with thorns, to whom homage was paid by mocking soldiers who crucified Him, a king who founds His empire on a cross, and whose subject are bound to Him with cords of love. Jesus is a better king and He calls us to come to Him. We can sympathize with Vashti's refusal to appear at Ahasueras' banquet when he called her, can't we? His was a calculating and demeaning summons. But Jesus is a king unlike any other. He loves His people, and His invitations to us are invitations of grace and mercy and hope. He is a King in whose rule we can rest securely, a Husband in whose love we can trust completely, and a Sovereign in whose power we can take refuge. Why refuse to come to Him when He calls?

2

Beauty and the Beast
(Esther 2:1-18)

Esther 2 is the Bible's Cinderella story. It is a romantic drama of which every Disney Princess would be proud. It features a beauty pageant in which the church girl wins the day and impresses everyone with her winning smile. What an example Esther is for little girls everywhere.

And in this way one of the worst abuses of scripture is perpetrated by well-meaning contemporary Bible readers. Esther 2, far from dripping with romance, is full of moral ambiguity and spiritual compromise. Esther 2, instead of offering us an example to follow, invites us to face the reality of life in which women are often objectified and made victims, where men can be predatory, and where, at least for some, fear is often more powerful than faith. Esther 2 is not an exciting episode of *Persia's Got Talent*. It is, rather, a dark and uncomfortable tale of abduction and abuse.

And yet, it is here, amidst all the moral ambiguities and shocking abuses that dog Esther's steps, that we are being invited to trace the footprints of the sovereign God, who is working in and through and despite the sin and suffering we find here, 'for the good of those who love him and are called according to his purpose' (Rom. 8:28). Esther 2 does not flinch from narrating for us the simple and ugly facts of life in ancient Persia where people are treated as commodities. It is no fairytale story of a poor Jewish girl falling in love with

97

Prince Charming. Esther 2 is a story the like of which, when we hear it on the news, we can scarcely bear to contemplate. There is no escapism here. Esther 2 is the real world.

And for some, that fact alone may prove to be extremely important, because it tells us that God's word speaks to the extremes of our experience, even when our society doesn't know what to say. The Lord is not confounded when the unthinkable happens. He is not silent when tragedy and sorrow and sin break in upon us and leave us broken. The prison of silence that can hold victims enslaved to shame and confusion is unlocked by passages like this one. The dark things we are unable to share with others are named here and faced here, by the God of wisdom and love. He has a Word for the abused and the abuser. He has something to say to the naive and the cynical. His Gospel is a real-world Gospel that works in the darkest realities of our lives. Esther 2, as bleak as it is, offers us unspeakable hope.

Back at the Court…
Back in chapter 1, remember, Ahasueras, drunk and enraged at the refusal of Queen Vashti to submit to the leering stares of the royal court, resolved to dismiss her, and find a new wife. As Chapter 2 opens, some time later, his anger is spent. And, we're told, he 'remembered Vashti' (2:1). Often in the Old Testament Scriptures, the language of *remembering* someone is used of God, to indicate His faithfulness to people over a period of time, as He purposes to show them mercy and kindness. He 'remembers people for good' (Neh. 5:19). But if something of that order is being indicated here, and if Ahasueras thinks of Vashti more positively, and with regret, our author is quick to add that the king also knows that he has been caught in his own impulsive folly. His decree to banish Vashti was irrevocable, and no matter the king's private feeling now, in the cold light of sobriety, he could not legally restore her.

And so he calls his advisors, who propose, verse 2, that a search be undertaken for the most beautiful women of the Empire, to be brought, like animals, to stock the king's harem. From among them, surely, there'd be one who could take Vashti's place? This plan, verse 4, 'pleased the king'.

Whatever pangs of remorse he felt for Vashti are forgotten now as his lust ignites afresh. It's a classic strategy of the un-renewed human heart, isn't it? Incapable of repentance, it can only *avoid* its guilt, it can *ignore* its guilt, it can *hide* its guilt beneath a blanket of indulgence, but it cannot ever really *remove* guilt. As many of us have discovered, only the blood of Jesus Christ can really do that.

1. A Tale of Exile: Strangers in a Strange Land

And as the curtain falls, for now, on Ahasueras, notice that it rises for the first time on one little Jewish family living in Susa. In 538 B.C., by decree of King Cyrus, much of the Jewish community had returned to Judah, a little over a generation before the events recorded in Esther. But many remained, scattered throughout the empire, having done as the prophet Jeremiah had counseled them (Jer. 29:6). They had settled down, and built homes and businesses. They had married and had given their children in marriage. This was now their home, and so they remained, exiles in a pagan land. Verses 5 and 6 make that point with some force. Literally they say something like, 'Now there was a Jew in Susa, the citadel, whose name was Mordecai… who had been *exiled* from Jerusalem among the *exiles* who were *exiled* with Jeconiah king of Judah, whom Nebuchadnezzar king of Babylon had *exiled*.' We get the message, don't we? Mordecai, and Esther his niece, are exiles. That is, though they *live* in Susa, they *belong* to the people of God, and that changes everything. They *are* strangers in a strange land, exiled, to be sure, but they are *not* cut off from the covenants of promise or the commonwealth of Israel. Whatever else happens, our author is saying, keep your eyes on this family. God is not done with His people yet.

So if verses 1-4 give us some insight into the casual and amoral brutality of the Persian court, here in verses 5-7 we have a very different picture. Here we see a covenant family struggling to survive. By all appearances, they have assimilated well into the host culture they inhabit. Mordecai is a pagan name meaning 'man of Marduk', the chief god of the Babylonian pantheon. Similarly, Esther's name probably references Ishtar, the goddess of love and war, though here she is introduced to us by her Hebrew name. She is, verse 7,

'Hadassah.' Orphaned at some point, she was adopted by Mordecai, who, according to verse 11, seems to have been utterly devoted to her. It's a household that has known tragedy, that has labored to accommodate to the culture while still tenaciously clinging to its roots. Esther's two names suggest the challenge facing the people of God in exile. To which world does she really belong? There are two Esthers: there is *Hadassah*, child of the covenant, citizen of the kingdom of God, and *Esther*, the pretty Persian girl, about to be swept up into a maelstrom of sorrow and responsibility she could never have imagined. How *do* they relate to one another? *Can* they be reconciled?

2. Between Two Worlds

And that is a dilemma that every member of the covenant community faces to this day. If we are Christians, we are called to be *in* the world but not *of* it. But many of us find ourselves with two identities, living double lives, uncertain how to bridge the gulf that lies between them. We feel keenly the reality of the social risks we take if we declare ourselves for Christ and begin to live accordingly. We feel just how powerful the pressure to conform to the pattern of this world really is. And so like Esther and Mordecai, we find ourselves caught on the horns of a dilemma, and we instinctively recognize that the path of obedience and faithfulness may be very costly indeed. Mordecai seems to sense that in verse 10 when he counsels Esther not to reveal her identity as a Jewish girl.

Sadly, it's counsel we recognize; a familiar strategy. We'll keep our heads down, let our lives be our testimony, and not let anyone know that we belong to Jesus. Learning how to live in the world while not belonging to it is hard and costly. But simply knowing that the hero and heroine of the book faced the same dilemma we encounter signals to us that God is not indifferent to the challenge.

3. Hapless and Helpless

And so now, the stage is at last set. And as the mighty resources of Persia swing into action to implement the king's decree, Esther's life is about to change forever. Susa is packed with young women gathered from across the empire, and placed under Hegai's care, all of them are about to compete for the position of queen. And Esther finds herself suddenly among them. Now understand that this was not a voluntary thing. It was not an open contest in search of the next *Miss Persia*. As the language of verse 8 hints at, Ahasueras gathered virgins into his harem under compulsion where necessary. Esther, we are told in verse 8, was '*taken* into the king's palace'. She did not fill out an application. Her life, and the lives of all the other young women in the harem, had been disrupted, as they were simply snatched from their homes to become the playthings of the king.

But it's not long before Esther wins the favor of Hegai who was in charge of the harem. She is given privileged status and benefits, as for the next year she and the other women are crimped and scraped and tweaked and beautified. And then, one by one, they were required to spend the night, each in turn, in the king's bed. As the story reaches its conclusion, Esther wins the throne, we learn, on the basis of her night with the king. Some try to exonerate Esther by suggesting that nothing happened that night between the king and Esther. Some blame Esther, accusing her of using sex as a tool to power. The truth is that Esther has been manipulated and abused. Emotionally and psychologically broken, she is a victim. We needn't amend the text to clean it up, nor should we scold Esther as though she were an ambitious modern starlet trying to sleep her way to a position of influence. Rather, we need to read these words with grief and empathy, recognizing in this story a tale that has been and continues to be repeated all over the world in every culture and in every age.

But as we take it all in, the ugliness and pain of it, we need to see that despite it all God was at work to build His kingdom. How does God build His kingdom in a world as dark as the one Esther 2 portrays?

(i) God makes even His enemies serve His ends
He uses wicked men and sinful deeds and thwarts their evil design and bends them to His own purposes. The 'young men' in verse 2, who come up with the plan that eventually leads to Esther's selection as queen, are described in the same language used to describe the prophet Samuel on the occasion

of his call. Their counsel is despicable, and yet, Esther tells us, their words, no less than Samuel's, become instruments in the execution of God's plan. They were like Caiaphas, the high priest, in John 11:51. He poured out only hatred and vitriol for Jesus when he argued that Christ should die for the people, not knowing that his words prophesied the very thing that would redeem God's church. So too, their wickedness notwithstanding, the advice of the king's counselors led to the positioning of Esther in the *only* place where she could save God's people. The crass and abusive contest for the queen's title was wicked to the core, and the suffering of those subjected to it should not be minimized. Yet the painful rise of Esther to the throne of Persia meant the salvation of the covenant people of God.

Consider the patriarch Joseph for a moment. If you were to ask him, after his enslavement and imprisonment and poverty and abuse, if those trials were anything other than evil, he would immediately say, 'Of course not.' And yet, when confronted with the very brothers who sold him into slavery, he could say with tears, 'What you intended for evil, God intended for good.' Undoubtedly, there is a great mystery here. But for anyone who has suffered at the hands of another, and who has begun to rest in God's sovereignty, it is nevertheless a precious truth, all its mystery notwithstanding: *what was intended for evil, God intended for good.*

(ii) God uses His weakest servants for His greatest works
So, first of all, we learn here that God makes even his enemies serve His ends. And then, secondly, we are being taught that God uses His weakest servants for His greatest works.

Notice that at the heart of God's design, and at the heart of the message of this chapter, stands Esther herself. Our eyes linger, not on the lust of Ahasueras, nor on the distress of his victims, nor on the opulence of the harem. Instead, our author has riveted our gaze upon Esther. In verses 1-4 we saw the callous and unfeeling power of the court of the king on full display, but then in verses 5-7 there is an abrupt contrast, isn't there? Here are Esther and Mordecai, with their broken home, struggling to work out how to sing the Lord's song in a strange land.

It is a study in contrasts. Amoral Ahasueras – all glory and riches and debauched power – and Esther: the very picture of weakness. An orphan. A woman. A Jew. It is a combination calculated to place her firmly on the margins, disenfranchised and outcast. She is taken, abducted, and forced into a life she would never choose. She has no power and no influence. And yet, who is it that God uses to accomplish His purposes and advance His kingdom? How is the kingdom of God built? Not by the mighty and the noble and the strong. Not by Ahasueras. Not by the powerbrokers and the culture shapers. Not by the influential and the impressive. God uses an abused, outcast girl, hiding her Judaism in abject fear. It is the weak things and the things that are not which God chooses to shame the wise and bring to nothing the things that are.

When we are tempted to think that the Kingdom of God advances because we can bankroll its ministries, because we can call on the great and the good to sponsor its causes; when we are tempted to believe that the politics of the world establish the kingdom of heaven, remember Esther.

In fact, it is precisely here, in her abject weakness and brokenness, a victim of the malice and hatred of the mighty and the political elites, it is *precisely here* that Esther preaches the gospel to us. It is here that she reminds us of Jesus Christ: the Lord of Glory who could, with a word, level His enemies, yet who was stripped and beaten and crucified, the One, who, though He was rich became poor, that by His poverty we might become rich (2 Cor. 8:9). Our Lord Jesus Christ redeems and saves and builds His church *by His Cross*. Esther 2 reminds us that God uses His weakest servants for His greatest works. It reminds us that Christ saves *by the Cross* and it teaches us that our lives, if they are to serve Him in response, must be cruciform too.

Martin Luther famously contrasted the theology of glory with the theology of the cross. By a theology of glory, he meant any approach to the Christian life that looks for outward displays of earthly power as its principle means for advancement. Instead, said Luther, *crux probat omnia* – the cross is the test of everything.

What of your life? Is it cruciform? Is it cross-shaped? Is it broken, dependent on God in Christ, by the Spirit? Is it self-effacing and God-exalting? Does it despair of earthly influence, yet in humility discover God's influence advanced? Esther 2 would teach us that God will bless and use such a life because it is a life that mirrors and echoes and looks like the life of Christ. This is the life to which Esther 2 is calling us.

God builds His kingdom in the real world of brokenness and sin and pain. He does it first by making even His enemies serve His ends. And He does it by using His weakest servants for His greatest works.

3

The Plot Thickens

(Esther 2:19–3:15)

'God's works of providence are his most holy, wise, and powerful preserving and governing all his creatures and all their actions.'[1] That is the helpful definition of the doctrine of providence provided by the Westminster Shorter Catechism. *Defining* providence, however, is *one* thing. *Discerning* providence at work, understanding the *design* of providence in our lives, *that is another thing entirely.* Many of us have come to that perplexing realization, often in the midst of very painful life events, that tracing out the complex web of divine intentionality, governing every event and every consequence, is simply beyond us, and we're left scratching our heads as we struggle to grasp what the Lord might be doing. As we saw when we looked at Esther 1, in the words of the Puritan pastor, John Flavel, 'Providence is like a Hebrew word. It is only understood when read backwards.' But even then, it is only ever understood partially and imperfectly.

Providence in Retrospect in the Everyday
When Mykal Riley's aunt was shot and killed by a mentally unstable gunman, everyone connected to the family must have wondered what God might be doing in this terrible tragedy. With the life insurance money his grandmother built him a

---

1. *Westminster Shorter Catechism* Question 11.

basketball court and there Riley learned to shoot hoops. About four years ago, Alabama were playing Mississippi State in an SEC basketball game in Atlanta, Georgia. State was in the lead, but Alabama had the ball and a chance to tie the game. It was Mykal Riley who took a shot from about 28 feet. Now I know *nothing* about American sports – which makes this illustration a risky business – but even I can appreciate the excitement and the tension of this moment. You can picture the scene, can't you? Everyone is on the edge of their seat. Riley takes the shot. The ball sails through the air, it hits the rim, it bounces around, thousands of hearts are now pounding in thousands of throats. The ball hits the backboard and goes in right at the buzzer to tie the game, sending it into overtime. Eight minutes later, a tornado came roaring past the Georgia Dome. 14,825 people who would otherwise have been walking outside in the path of the tornado after the game concluded were instead safely inside the dome. It literally was a lifesaving shot.

What was God doing that day when Mykal Riley's aunt was shot and killed? We can't possibly know all the ways He worked in and through it in His wisdom and for His own glory. But one of the things we *can* say for sure He *was* doing was shaping and molding a young man and directing his steps so that he might throw a ball that would save many lives. When the bullet left the gunman's weapon no-one could have foreseen that among the various consequences for good and ill, such an outcome was part of God's master plan. But it was. Such is the mystery of the providence of God.[2]

Providence in Retrospect in Esther
Just as we can read a portion of God's purpose in Riley's life, though only in retrospect, we can do so also here in the book of Esther, as we turn our attention to the end of chapter 2 and then chapter 3. We are at last in a position to begin to trace out something of what God was about when Esther was taken from her home and forced into the life of a concubine in the harem of Ahasueras, King of Persia. In the last chapter, Hadassah, the pretty Jewish peasant girl, was swept up into the maelstrom of public life and crowned Esther, Queen of

2. www.si.com/vault/2009/03/16/105787321/the-shot-that-saved-lives.

Persia. Now we look at the next major section of the book of Esther, which begins in chapter 3. But before we do, notice that, in 2:19-23, nestled between the account of Esther's coronation and the introduction of Haman in chapter 3, we have a little vignette, a snapshot of court life, that reveals for us something of the Machiavellian, cut-throat character of the political scene in the citadel of Susa.

Look at 2:19-23. Mordecai now appears to serve in some capacity as a civil servant – that is the significance of him 'sitting in the king's gate' – where he uncovers the plot of the disaffected eunuchs, Bigthan and Teresh, who conspire to assassinate Ahasueras. Presumably through mediators, Mordecai was able pass word to Esther, who, in turn, warned the king. After investigation is made, Bigthan and Teresh are caught red-handed and summarily executed. Through all the drama of chapter 2, as Esther is taken from the home of her adoptive father Mordecai, and made to live in the harem and treated as a plaything of the king, through all the horror and heartache of that perplexing situation we have been asking, 'What is God doing?' Well, now we know *one* of the things He was doing. In His providence, 'upholding and governing all his creatures and all their actions', *He has brought Esther and Mordecai to the place where they are the only ones able to rescue the king.*

1. Chaotic Mess or Divine Design?

When I was in art school as an undergraduate, in the textiles department there were a number of students learning to weave the most amazing tapestries on huge looms. When viewed from the reverse, a tapestry like that is a chaotic mass of loose, multicolored threads hanging down from the various places where they have been woven. Viewed from that perspective, it is impossible to make out *any* order or design at all, but when it is complete and you view the tapestry from the other side, each thread is finally seen in its relation to all the others, woven together into a coherent whole that makes perfect sense, full of beauty, leaving us to marvel at the skill of the weaver. *That* is the providence of God. Our view is like looking at a loom from behind. It seems random and chaotic and incoherent. Viewed from the perspective of God the master weaver, each thread of each life is being woven together according to a perfect design into an amazing tapestry that will, at its completion, make us all adore the wisdom of the heavenly Artist. God works all things together, every thread, the dark and sore ones, as well as the bright and happy ones, for the good of those who love Him and are called according to His purpose.

And so, in verse 23, a careful record of Mordecai's intervention on the king's behalf was made for posterity. Now it may help you to learn that the Persian monarchs were known not only for the bloody and amoral nature of their use of power – and we've seen plenty of that in the story so far, haven't we? – but they were also known for the extravagant and swift generosity with which they rewarded those who served them. But the point here is that Mordecai, *who saved the king's life*, goes *un*rewarded. And that sets us up to feel the biting irony in what happens next. Look at chapter 3.

Mordecai saved the king, remember. The king ensured that a permanent record of his heroic action was made so that *no-one* would ever forget…and *Haman the Agagite* gets promoted. In verse 2, everyone bows to Haman, everyone that is, except Mordecai, whose unbent neck becomes the target of Haman's relentless hatred. Did you spot the same language used to describe Bigthan and Teresh and *their* murder plot in 2:21 being used again of Haman in 3:5 and 6? Filled with anger the King's eunuchs sought to 'lay their hands on him'. Full of rage Haman had a similar design, only this time a conspiracy to just kill one man wasn't nearly enough to satisfy his hunger for revenge. Haman's plan becomes a 'final solution' aimed at the genocide of the Jewish people. He wants nothing short of ethnic cleansing. You see the irony? Having saved Ahasueras from the *lesser* evil, Mordecai and Esther fall foul of the *greater* evil. *Ahasueras* gets rescued, while his *rescuers* fall into the very danger the king had faced, only on a much larger scale. Talk about sudden reversals. It's dizzying.

Living as the People of God in a Dark World
And as we try to take it all in, don't we find ourselves repeating on behalf of Mordecai and Esther a line that often appears on our lips, as we wrestle with God's providence: 'It's just not fair'? But that is part of the point. The author *wants* us to feel

something of the very frustration that Mordecai and Esther must have wrestled with as this whole thing unfolded. 'It's just plain wrong.' our author wants us to say. This is not unbiased reporting. God has a point of view that He wants us to share. We are being turned against Haman and made to root for Mordecai, because the Bible wants to change the arithmetic by which we evaluate the relative importance of people and things. We are being made to cheer for Mordecai and Esther and look in contempt at vain Ahasueras and horror at brutal Haman. We are being taught to stand in solidarity with the people of God and to sever our allegiances to the priorities of the world. Even the way the story of Esther is retold aims to subvert the world's values and transform our lives by the renewal of our minds. As chapter 3 develops we watch with horrified fascination as cold and calculating Haman carefully schemes and plots. He casts Pur, that is, he casts lots in a superstitious mockery of religion, not knowing the lessons we are beginning to learn, that neither pagan deities nor blind chance govern all things but the sovereign hand of the living God. We know, what Haman does not, that 'The lot is cast into the lap, but its every decision is from the LORD' (Prov. 16:33). Even the superstition and malice of Haman are superintended and bounded by the decree of God. When the twelfth month arrived, Haman finally takes action. Look at what he tells Ahasueras.

First, he says that the Jewish people do not keep the king's laws *but live by another law*. He is appealing to the king's pride and implying Jewish indifference to the omnipotent might of the monarch's decrees. And then, secondly, he says in verse 8, '*it is not to the king's profit to tolerate them.*' Haman really knows where to aim his darts, doesn't he? He draws a bead on Ahasueras' self-interest. Everyone and everything in the empire exists for the profit and pleasure of the king, but not these traitorous Jews. Don't tolerate them. He offers to pay 100,000 talents of silver. That's about 750,000 pounds of silver, to bankroll what would be an empire-wide pogrom, the likes of which could only be compared to the Holocaust. The king, for his part, gives Haman his signet ring, vesting in him virtually limitless authority to act in his name. Everything is placed in Haman's hands. All the resources are freely given to do with as he sees fit. In verses 12-15 the administrative machinery swings into motion as the vast bureaucracy of the empire implements Haman's plan. Messages are sent in every language to every corner of the empire with the news that the Jews are to be 'destroyed, killed and annihilated', eleven months later, on the thirteenth day of the month of Adar (3:13). As the citadel of Susa is thrown into an uproar at the news, the whole episode ends with Haman and Ahasueras enjoying a few beers after a hard day's plotting. It is a chilling story that would be hard to believe, were it not for Auschwitz and Rwanda and Kosovo and Sudan.

The providence of God is very much to the fore as the history of Esther now begins to pick up pace. And yet we are forced to see that God's providence does not cushion His people from trials nor from the malice of evil men. Esther 3 does not resolve the mysteries involved in the question of how God's sovereignty and the reality of evil relate. But neither will it let us ignore the fact that even the evil of Haman is bounded and superintended by God's most holy, wise and powerful upholding and governance. In fact, Esther 3 tells us that, God's sovereignty notwithstanding, we live in a world of conflict, a dark world, where belonging to the people of God makes one a target.

2. Two principles for survival in a dark world
But as it tells us all that, I want you to notice that it also provides two resources to help us live in such a world. Here are two principles for survival in a hostile environment.

(i) Know the nature of the conflict
Did you notice that Haman is almost never *simply* Haman? He is Haman the *Agagite*. In 3:10 he is 'Haman, son of Hammedatha, the Agagite, *the enemy of the Jews*.' We are being tipped off, do you see, to what is really going on between Haman and Mordecai? Here's why Mordecai won't bow to Haman. Here's why Haman wants *genocide*, not *justice*. Haman is an Agagite. Agag, you may recall, was the King of the Amalekites, over whom God had pronounced a sentence of destruction in 1 Samuel 15. Israel's first king, Saul, refused to obey and spared Agag, who was eventually slain by the prophet Samuel. *Haman* is a descendant of *Agag*.

But Mordecai and Esther belong to the tribe of Benjamin, *the tribe from which King Saul came*. This is, in other words, another round of an age-old conflict, not simply between two warring ethnic groups, but between the kingdom of God and the kingdom of Satan, between the Seed of the Woman and the seed of the Serpent, between the reign of Christ and the reign of antichrist. It is the same battle that continues to rage to this day. 'Our adversary,' ultimately, is 'the devil, who prowls around like a roaring lion seeking someone to devour' (1 Pet. 5:8). We wrestle 'not against flesh and blood, but against principalities and powers and against spiritual hosts of wickedness in heavenly places' (Eph. 6:11-12). It is *his* schemes against which we must stand firm. 'Friendship with the world is enmity against God' (James 4:4).

Friends, there is a war on. As God's people in every age live, as Haman said of the Jews in his day, according to *other* laws than the laws of the empire, they live by the law of God, and according to His norms, there will be *opposition*. But Esther 2 and 3 wants us to see the true nature of that opposition – it is *spiritual* and it has been raging since our first father Adam ate the forbidden fruit. But as we do, let's remember that we do not stand in the same place Esther and Mordecai did in that conflict. We stand in the age of fulfillment: the Seed of the Woman has come and crushed the Serpent's head. He has made public spectacle of the principalities and power, having triumphed over them in the cross (Col. 2:15). The battle rages hotly, so let us be prepared, dressed in the full armor of God. But the battle has already been won by our Lord Jesus Christ, so let us take courage and stand firm.

(ii) Know the end from the beginning
And then, Esther 2 and 3 teaches us to *know the end from the beginning*. That is the message of the snapshot of court life provided in 2:19-23. It tells the whole story of Esther in microcosm, up front. Before the storm of chapter 3 begins to break, we get to see in advance God's final goal. Esther and Mordecai face all they face and are where they are in the sovereign arrangement of almighty God so that they might be saviors. Here is a murder plot and only they can thwart it. That is who this unlikely pair really are, our author is saying.

Don't forget that, as the dark clouds of terrible evil begin to gather overhead. They are saviors. We get to glimpse the end of the story before the real drama gets underway.

Keep in view the bright destiny into which the Lord your God will bring you. Keep it before your gaze as the darkness descends, and opposition comes, and suffering overtakes you.

That is what we see our Savior doing, isn't it, as He faces the horror of the cross? It was, as Hebrews 12:2 says, 'for the joy that was set before him' that the Lord Jesus 'endured the cross, despising the shame' and is now 'seated at the right hand of the throne of God'. We are taught that same principle in Romans 8:18ff. There Paul writes: 'I consider that the sufferings of this present time are not worth comparing with the glory that is to be revealed to us…. For we know that the whole creation has been groaning together in the pains of childbirth until now. And not only the creation, but we ourselves, who have the firstfruits of the Spirit, groan inwardly as we wait eagerly for adoption as sons, the redemption of our bodies. For in this hope we were saved. Now hope that is seen is not hope. For who hopes for what he sees? But if we hope for what we do not see, we wait for it with patience.'

Keep your eyes on the end, and you will be able to endure the means. We groan inwardly. But our present sufferings are not worth comparing to the glory to be revealed. We can endure groaning if we keep glory in view. Esther 2:19-23 reminds us that God has already told us the whole story. We know how history ends. The Lamb who was slain is the Lion of the tribe of Judah who reigns over all. We who have been bought with the blood of the cross are kept by the power of God unto salvation ready to be revealed at the last time. Know the end from the beginning.

There is conflict, a clash of kingdoms, a confrontation between righteousness and wickedness, holiness and sin, truth and error, the reign of Christ and the rule of antichrist. We are locked in a real spiritual battle, but we know what the Hamans of this world do not. We know that the war has already been won. Christ has died and risen, and is now Lord over all, and one day He will bring the battle to its end. The new heavens and the new earth will come and the Lamb will wipe away every tear from our eyes.

4

For Such a Time as This

(Esther 4:1-17)

Think for a moment about the defining moments of your life; those forks in the road that set your course and determined your future; moments when you made a choice and turned a corner and declared your purpose and set your face and marked out your territory. Some of them are moments, not of choice, but of happenstance: the biopsy result, the stock market change, the company merger. Defining moments shape us and direct our steps in ways that leave us utterly changed.

As we turn to Esther 4 we come to the pivot of the whole book. In terms of character development, Esther moves from a subordinate and secondary role in the narrative, meekly following Mordecai's instructions, to the primary and central role in the story, so that by verse 17, 'Mordecai then went away and did everything as Esther had ordered him.' For Queen Esther *personally* it was also a defining moment. A crucial decision had to be made, and only she can make it, upon which hung the fate, not just of her own broken family, but of her entire people. It was a decisive moment for Esther and for the Jewish people, and one of the key things it will help us begin to come to terms with is the oftentimes complex intersection of two vitally important biblical themes: the absolute sovereignty of God in providence, 'upholding and governing all his creatures and all their actions,' *and* the

113

absolute responsibility of human beings as His creatures in their respective vocations and callings. The sovereignty of God governs and directs all things, including our free actions and decisions, and yet, Esther 4 teaches us, our responsibilities cannot be denied by appeal to God's sovereignty. As Queen Esther discovers, the sovereignty of God does not get us off the hook when called to make difficult choices.

You will recall from chapter 3 that Haman the Agagite, the enemy of the Jews, in his rage against Mordecai, has manipulated the amoral King Ahasueras into sanctioning the genocide of the Jewish people throughout the Empire. Eleven months later, on the thirteenth day of the month of Adar, they were all to be, in the words of Haman's decree, 'killed, destroyed and annihilated.' Chapter 3 ended with the citadel of Susa in an uproar while Ahasueras and Haman, wearied from a hard day plotting genocide, unwind over a few cocktails. As chapter 4 opens, like a CNN news segment, we cut immediately to 'get the reaction on the ground'. The camera zooms in on Mordecai, tearing his clothes, putting on sackcloth and ashes and loudly proclaiming his distress and grief throughout the city of Susa. And then in verse 3, one can almost hear the news anchor back in the studio – 'those are scenes repeated across the empire: in every province, wherever the king's command and his decree reached, there was great mourning among the Jews, with fasting and weeping and lamenting, and many of them lay in sackcloth and ashes.'

Esther, however, appears to have been oblivious to Haman's plot and the uproar outside the palace grounds. When she turned on the news that evening and saw images of Mordecai weeping at the palace gates, she is understandably concerned. She sends a change of clothes to Mordecai, and eventually sends Hathach, one of her servants, to find out exactly what was going on. And in verses 6-9 Mordecai gives Hathach a detailed report of all that had taken place and begins to plead with Esther to intercede on behalf of her people before the king. In verse 11 we have Esther's reply: 'All the king's servants and the people of the king's provinces know that if any man or woman goes to the king inside the inner court without being called, there is but one law – to be put to death, except the one to whom the king holds out the golden scepter so that he may live. But as for me, I have not been called to come in to the king these thirty days.'

It's not hard to picture the blood draining from Esther's face as she hears Mordecai's suggestion. 'Doesn't he understand what he's asking? To go in to the king uninvited is to risk one's life, to gamble upon the capricious whimsy of an amoral tyrant, and if you think I'm the ideal candidate, you should know that the king hasn't wanted to see me for about a month now. I'm not so sure your plan's such a good idea, Mordecai.'

1. The Uncomfortable Choice

And in verses 12-17 we have what is by far the most famous passage in the book of Esther. Mordecai's reply is a master class in balancing equally ultimate truths, helping us to hold together crucial principles without compromise. First, in verse 13, he says Esther faces *an uncomfortable choice*: 'Do not think to yourself that in the king's palace you will escape any more than all the other Jews.'

Mordecai is unflinching in shattering the secret refuge of Esther's heart, isn't he? 'Do not think that because you are the queen that your identity will remain hidden for long. If the Jews die in the pogrom Haman is planning, you will surely die with them, queen or not.' He is forcing a decision that Esther has so far managed to avoid. Remember that she is the one character in this story with two names. She is Hadassah, the Jewish peasant girl. And she is Esther, the Persian beauty and royal consort to the most powerful man in the world. For some years now, since she first came to the harem, she has lived a life submerged beneath Persian culture, her Jewish roots utterly hidden and obscured. But now she can't live that way for long. There is no belonging to the people of God, while living like a child of the world. There is no way to be a secret Christian and a public pagan. Esther is going to have to choose. And so are we.

You're connecting the dots, aren't you? The application from this text is evident. Perhaps God is calling *you* to recognize that the double life you have been living simply cannot go on. Jesus said, 'No one can serve two masters, for either he will hate the one and love the other, or he will be devoted to the one and despise the other' (Matt. 6:24). 'Whoever is not with me is against me, and whoever does not gather with me scatters' (Matt. 12:30). There is no middle ground, no neutral territory, no demilitarized zone within which you may safely sign a truce with sin.

Whose are you? Jesus Christ claims your allegiance, and He calls you to face the cost of discipleship. We are to pick up our cross and follow Him, and then be prepared to lose our life for His sake that we might find it (Matt. 10:38-39). It is hard, and it is scary, and there will be a cost to be paid, Esther. But you belong to the covenant people of God and it is time you stood in solidarity with them. There is no defecting from the kingdom of Jesus Christ.

2. The Unshakeable Hope

The second thing Mordecai tells Esther points, not to *her identity*, but to *his own security*. If, first of all, we learn here about *the uncomfortable choice* we must make to stand for the cause of Jesus Christ, we also learn secondly about *the unshakeable hope* that those who do so can enjoy.

The book of Esther is a small room in the center of which sits a huge elephant, never mentioned yet obvious to all. The elephant in the room is of course the presence and sovereign grace of Almighty God. Here in Esther 4:14, the elephant that had been sitting meekly in the room now shuffles over to sit right in our laps. If we hadn't noticed it before we can't miss it now. Look at Mordecai's words in verse 14: 'For if you keep silent at this time, *relief and deliverance will rise for the Jews from another place,* but you and your father's house will perish.'

Relief and deliverance will arise from another place. Mordecai is full of unshakeable hope and security, isn't he? He is facing the extermination of his entire people at the hands of an ancestral enemy, Haman the Agagite. The never-to-be-repealed decree of Ahasueras, King of the Persian Empire, has proclaimed their destruction. And Mordecai, along with his people, has been swept up in grief as a result. But it was *not* despair that characterized the Jewish reaction to Haman's decree. Look back again at verse 3: 'There was a

great mourning among the Jews with fasting, weeping and
lamenting.' That language appears again, word for word, in
Joel 2:12-14 which is a call from God to His people to 'return
to me with all your heart, *with fasting, with weeping, and with
mourning*; and rend your hearts and not your garments.'
Almost certainly, the author of Esther 4 wants us to read the
reaction of the Jews in light of Joel 2 as a response, not of
despair, but of repentant faith returning to the Lord. 'Return
to the LORD your God,' Joel goes on, 'for he is gracious and
merciful, slow to anger, and abounding in steadfast love; and
he relents over disaster. *Who knows* whether he will not turn
and relent, and leave a blessing behind him?' Do you see
the echo of Joel 2:14 in Mordecai's words in the second half
of Esther 4:14: '*Who knows* but that you have come to the
kingdom for such a time as this?'

Where does Mordecai get his security and the unshakeable
hope that characterizes him before the hatred of Haman and
the near absolute power of the king? Mordecai knows the
promises of God. Mordecai knows the covenant faithfulness
of the Lord who has sworn to relent when His people turn
back to Him. Relief and deliverance will arise from another
place. Mordecai rests secure in the sovereign faithfulness of
the covenant-keeping God whose promises never fail. He
trusts that the Lord, who reigns over Haman's wicked heart
and Ahasueras' perverted power and Esther's fear-filled
mind, also rules the destiny of His people and has promised
to deliver them when they call upon Him in faith.

Here is the proper use of the doctrine of divine sovereignty.
It is not a theological bludgeon with which to beat other
Christians. It is not a shibboleth by which to test for orthodoxy.
It is a refuge in which to rest secure, a safe harbor in which
to anchor your faith amidst every trial, a hiding place in the
storm. Mordecai knows that God, because He is Lord over
all things, utterly and comprehensively and exhaustively
sovereign, will not, cannot, fail to keep His promises and
uphold His covenant. Relief and deliverance will arise from
another quarter. The sovereignty and faithfulness of God is
the scriptural medicine for the disease of fear. You kill the
germ of anxiety with a hefty dose of divine sovereignty.
Brothers and sisters, your life rests in the hand of the God of

infinite faithfulness, goodness and grace, and you could not be safer, nor more secure.

It may also be the case that Mordecai wants Esther to understand that although there is a responsibility she is being called upon to face up to here, there is also a danger she must be careful to avoid. The danger to be avoided is thinking herself essential, even indispensable. Isn't that a real temptation we sometimes face? We either avoid our duty, using God's sovereignty as a justification for our passivity, or we step up to our obligations and, if we are not careful, we begin to minimize our dependence on the Lord, thinking ourselves to be the one vital cog in the machine, the indispensable component in God's plan. It is a trap Satan loves to ensnare God's people with. If he cannot paralyze us into inactivity, or leave us passive with distorted views of God's sovereignty, he will make us overstate our own importance and make us bear the weight of the responsibility for the salvation of others entirely on our own, so minimizing God's role, and maximizing ours.

Frankly, were it not for the truth Mordecai declares so boldly here, I could never climb the pulpit steps. If I believed that God were not sovereign in the salvation of sinners; if I thought that their destiny rested entirely on the exercise of their wills and thus also on my ability to persuade them and influence them and sway them; if that is how I thought, I would not be standing before them preaching the Word of God. Instead, I would be cowering in a darkened room somewhere, overwhelmed at the unbearable burden of that obligation. No. Praise God that salvation belongs to the Lord. Their redemption is not my responsibility. I am not called to save sinners. I am called to preach Christ. It is God alone who saves. And far from paralyzing us in our efforts to make Christ known, that truth frees us to do it boldly and without fear. Relief and deliverance will arise from another place. If you don't go in to the king, Esther, do not think that your failure to fulfill that duty will somehow derail God's plan and place it beyond recovery. Our salvation does not rest on you but on God. Salvation belongs to the Lord. Praise God that that is true. What a relief. What an incentive to serve Him with boldness. Relief and deliverance will arise from another place.

3. The Unavoidable Duty

There is an uncomfortable choice we must make, and an unshakable hope we can enjoy, and then finally, in the second half of verse 14, Mordecai tells Esther that there is *an unavoidable duty we must fulfill.* Look at the text, 'Who knows whether you have not come to the kingdom for such a time as this?'

Review your own history, Esther. See the steps that led you here. Haven't you asked yourself so often, through all the heartbreak and sorrow of those days, what God was doing? Could it be that you have come to the kingdom for just this moment? You are in a unique place in the providence of God, with unique opportunities and responsibilities. Don't you see the duty that rests upon you to which you are now being called? You are God's instrument for such a time as this.

It is a question worth asking ourselves, isn't it? For what has God brought me to this moment and to this place? Who has He made me to be, in His wise providence? What are the unique opportunities that I have, arising from the peculiar web of relationships I have developed? How is the path of duty illumined for me by the overruling sovereignty of God at work in my life? Those were very much the kinds of questions Mordecai was asking Esther to begin to wrestle with.

And as verses 15 and 16 make very clear, they were questions that did not wait long for an answer. Esther resolves her fears. She makes her choice. She opts for solidarity with the people of God no matter what waits for her by way of consequence. She calls the people of God to continue fasting in earnest, this time with a view specifically to God's provision for her, and she will join them as together they wait upon the Lord for the next three days. And then, in verse 16, comes Esther's immortal declaration: 'I will go to the king, though it is against the law, and if I perish, I perish.' It is the decisive moment, not just in the narrative, nor even in Esther's life, but in the life of God's people at this point in salvation history.

For Such a Time as This: From Queen Esther to King Jesus
And as Esther's words ring in our ears, resounding with notes of courage and faith and heroism, it's hard not to hear in them an echo of another Savior's words, spoken at the

greatest decisive moment of them all. In the garden, staring into the gloom of Calvary, the submission and resolve we see in Esther are surpassed and fulfilled in the One to whom she points us, as the Lord Jesus Christ prayed to His Father in heaven, 'If it be possible, let this cup pass from me. Yet not my will, but yours be done.' Like Esther, in the citadel of Susa and for the exiled Jews of the Empire, so now for God's elect in every place and in every age, at just the right time (Rom. 5:6), in the fullness of time (Gal. 4:4), *for just such a time as this*, God has raised up a Savior, in His Son, the Lord Jesus Christ. But whereas Esther risked all to intercede for her people, we have a better Mediator, one who did not merely risk all, but who laid it all down and died for His people. What Esther confessed as a possibility, Jesus owned and chose as a necessity, for us and for our salvation. He died that we might live.

Esther 4 directs our gaze to the great decisive moment where salvation was won. And it calls each of us to a decisive moment of our own. Has God in His sovereign purpose brought you to this place for such a time as this, that you might hear the gospel of Jesus Christ? Will you join the people of God in Esther 4 in repentance for their sin, rending the hearts and not their garments, and find refuge, in Jesus Christ alone, who has gone before the throne of glory for us, that we might live?

5

Gallows Humor
(Esther 5)

It is often said that God has a sense of humor. Usually we're referring to some ironic twist of providence, some unexpected consequence that taught us the very lesson we needed to learn at precisely the time we needed to learn it. We mean some missed opportunity that led to the very thing we hoped for in the end, only better. God delights to shower His grace upon us, sometimes directly, but often obliquely. He loves to surprise His children and make them laugh in sheer delight at the discovery that the folly of God is wiser than man's wisdom. One place where the wit of God can be seen quite clearly is Esther 5.

Haman the Agagite has contrived to have his murderous intention towards the Jews become an empire-wide policy, signed into law with the royal seal of Ahasueras himself. In chapter 4, Mordecai prevailed upon Esther to face up to her responsibility, indeed her divine calling, to go in to the king uninvited to plead for her people, risking her life in the process. Esther, who had gone incognito for so long, now resolves at last to identify fully with God's covenant people. And as the chapter ends she calls a fast – in which she herself will participate – as the church of God in Susa intercedes on Esther's behalf and for their own deliverance. After three days of fasting Esther will go in to the king, declaring, in words that have rung down the ages in the truest tones of heroism, 'If I perish, I perish.'

A Tale of Contrasts

When I was a boy they showed black and white reruns of the Lone Ranger on TV on Saturday mornings. Each week would end with a cliffhanger, and I'd have to wait a whole week for the next episode. When Saturday morning came around I was desperate to know what was going to happen. Chapter 4 rather left us with a cliffhanger, didn't it? And so as we come to chapter 5 we are eager to find out how things will go for Queen Esther and her risky visit to the king. But I want to make sure that, in our haste to find out what will happen next, you do not miss one of the wonderful features of our text. Part of the author's intention here is not simply to recount the facts, but to make us laugh at the glorious ironies that adorn those facts. Notice how, instead of cutting to the chase and immediately telling us how it all turns out for Esther and her people, the author himself slows everything down. Every detail of the events in the throne room of the king is recorded in painstaking precision, as though to invite us not to rush things, but, as if savoring a fine wine, to enjoy the tale; to roll the delicious wit of God over our palettes to be sure we get the full flavor. The general title for our study in Esther, is 'Sudden Reversals', and there are several reversals here, all unexpected and glorious, displaying for us God's goodness, and the folly of human pride, in a way intended to make us relish every minute of the story, and leave us chuckling in wonder at the perfect wisdom of our Sovereign Lord. To help us begin to see some of that, I want you to notice three contrasts in Esther 5. First in verses 1-3 we find *life, not death*. Secondly in verses 4-8 we find *a queen, not a criminal*. And in verses 9-14 we meet *folly, not wisdom*.

1. Life, Not Death

First, in verses 1-3, we meet *life, not death*. Gone is the racy switching back and forth between Mordecai and Esther that characterized the prose of chapter 4. Now we are introduced to a carefully staged scene in which every single detail is described. If we were looking for an immediate resolution to the cliff-hanger at the end of chapter 4, we'll be disappointed. What we get instead is a slow motion shot. Look at it. Esther selects the royal robe for her ordeal. Esther *stands*, we learn.

Then we are told *where*: the inner court, carefully positioned in front of the king's quarters. Then, once Esther is in place, the camera cuts to the throne room. Inside the king is *sitting*. Note carefully there the contrast with Esther. He is on the *royal throne*. She is the supplicant. He holds the power. He is inside the *throne room*, notice. Oh, and the throne room is *opposite* the entrance to the palace... 'Enough already.', we want to cry. 'Will you get on with it and tell us what is going to happen.'

But the frustration and the tension we are feeling are all part of the author's plan. He has us right where he wants us. The tension is palpable. Ominous violins play in the background as we tremble with Esther, almost holding our breath waiting for the moment when, in verse 2, Ahasueras looks up… and *there she is.* Esther has positioned herself, in all her royal finery, so that she would be framed perfectly in the doorway, directly opposite the throne. The king has not seen her for more than thirty days now. But there she stands, waiting, risking everything to see him. Now, we know from carvings found at the ancient palace at Persepolis that behind the throne of Ahasueras stood a Median soldier with a huge axe. So the king can see Esther, striking a pose, dramatically framed in the doorway, but *Esther* can also see the throne, and all the trappings of power, with the evening sun glinting on the axe-man's blade held high, poised for action.

This is it. All the prayers of the people of God have been concentrated on this moment. Note verse 2: 'And when the king saw Queen Esther standing in the court, she won favor in his sight, and he held out to Esther the golden scepter that was in his hand. Then Esther approached and touched the tip of the scepter.' Life, not death. Mercy, not condemnation. Hope replaces fear. She wins favor in his sight. God is at work, inclining the heart of the king and blessing His covenant child. Ahasueras holds out the golden scepter and she lives. The terror she must have felt only moments before is gone. The Lord has heard the cries of His people and answered.

Believing Prayer: The Corollary of Confidence
in the Sovereignty of God
And that, surely, is a major part of the message of this text: God loves to hear the cries of His children. For three days they

fasted and sought the Lord, repenting and returning to Him and interceding on Esther's behalf. And here, at least in part, is the answer of heaven. Favor, not condemnation. Acceptance, not rejection. Life, not death. God loves to hear the cries of His children. Remember the exhortation of Jesus: 'If you, being evil, know how to give good gifts to your children, *how much more will your Father in heaven give good things to those who ask him.*' (Matt. 7:11 NKJV). That's the point. Believing prayer is the necessary corollary of confidence in the sovereignty of God. Let me say that again, *believing prayer is the necessary corollary of confidence in the sovereignty of God*. If you really believe that God the Lord reigns, that He governs all things, which is the message of the book of Esther over and over again, if you really believe that, then you will *pray boldly. Believing prayer is the necessary corollary of confidence in the sovereignty of God*. In the words of the great Calvinistic Baptist missionary to India, William Carey, if you embrace and rest in God's sovereignty, you will 'expect great things from God and attempt great things for God'. That is what Esther did. She expected great things from God and did great things for Him. And the Lord answered with blessing and favor.

(Another) Heroic Deliverance from Death
Interestingly the Jewish Midrash (a kind of commentary) on this passage highlights the Jews' three days of fasting under the threat of death, and the way God answered. It declared, 'Israel [is] never left in dire distress more than three days.'[1] And then it pointed to Hosea 6:2: 'After two days he will revive us; on the third day he will raise us up, that we may live before him.' That is what is happening in Esther 5. Three days under the shadow of death and on the third, not death, but life. Which, of course, is immensely suggestive of Another, upon whose shoulders the duty of acting on behalf of the people of God fell. The heroism of Esther in the throne room of Ahasueras, as dramatic as it was, pales before the heroic deliverance from death won for the whole people of God by the Lord Jesus Christ, who was, 'delivered for our trespasses

---

1. Cited in Karen H. Jobes, *Esther, NIVAPC* (Grand Rapids, MI: Zondervan 1999), p. 146.

and, on the third day, raised for our justification' (Rom. 4:25). Life, not death. That is what He won for all who trust in Him.

Esther's story is a shadow of the One to come, who does far more than she. *Esther* wins favor and is *spared* unjust condemnation. But *Jesus*, who was not guilty, was nevertheless made the object of divine wrath and *was* condemned. *Esther* lived, but *Jesus* died that *we* might live. Esther merely *risked* all, and won through. *Jesus* actually *gave* all, and He did so, not simply *for* us. He did it *instead* of us. He died, the just for the unjust, to bring us to God. That is the good news we have. Apart from faith in Jesus we are guilty before God and under a sentence of death. But Jesus died that guilty sinners like us might live. The golden scepter was held out to Esther as she acted on behalf of her people. Esther was spared. But Jesus was not spared. He *died* for His people at the cross. The good news is that the sentence has been fulfilled, the penalty satisfied, for anyone who trusts in the Lord Jesus Christ, so if you have not done so, believe on the Lord Jesus Christ and you will be saved. And for those who *do* trust in Christ, as Hebrews 4:16 says, we need never fear coming before the One seated on heaven's throne in condemnation again. No, now we can go to the throne of grace boldly, with confidence, 'to receive mercy and find grace to help in time of need.'

2. Queen, not Criminal

Then, secondly, look at verses 4-8. Not only does Esther receive *life and not death*, but she is acclaimed *queen, not treated as a criminal*. Having held out the royal scepter, and preserved her life, the king is full of curiosity. 'What is it, Queen Esther? What is your request? It shall be given you, even up to half of my kingdom' (v. 3). What in the world would move you to risk your neck to come to the throne room without an invite, Esther? And in her answer Esther displays a calculating side to her character we have not yet encountered. It is hard not to admire her courage here. Who talks to the king like this. He demands an answer, and she bats her eyelashes and obfuscates. Instead, she says, 'Come to my party.' *Now* she's talking Ahasueras' language, right? Remember the opulent soirées in chapters 1 and 2? We can almost hear the vacant-headed monarch exclaim, like a character from a P. G. Woodhouse novel, 'A party. What fun. Run and fetch Haman immediately.'

Then, later, full of wine and feeling magnanimous, and still no doubt burning with curiosity about Esther's request, the king *repeats* his offer: 'What do you want? You can have anything up to half my kingdom.' (v. 6). Now watch Esther. Like a hunter skillfully luring her prey into the trap, she *almost* tells all, but not quite. 'My wish and my request is...' – the king leans forward expectantly – 'come to my party again tomorrow, and bring Haman along too, and I'll tell you everything.' It was a dangerous game, to be sure, but now there's *no way* Ahasueras can refuse, can he? He's just *got to know*. The suspense must have been killing him, freshly beguiled as he was by Esther's charms. You see what's happening? Ahasueras and Haman are being mocked. Who holds the power? Not the emperor nor his bloodthirsty right-hand man, Haman. It's *Esther,* the Jewish peasant girl. She has the mightiest ruler in the world and his lackey eating out of the palm of her hand. What a delightful reversal that is. The peasant girl really has become queen.

Actually, Esther is only called queen once before now in the whole book. But after *this* moment, she is Queen Esther sixteen times more. In fact, since 2:22, in obedience to the instructions of Mordecai, she has done all she could to assimilate to the life of a royal consort living in the harem of Ahasueras. She has submerged her identity as Hadassah, the member of God's covenant people, beneath her Persian alter-ego, Esther. And yet, as she tells us in 4:11, her best efforts notwithstanding, the king has not called for her presence in over a month. He seems to have grown bored with her, so that the more she sought to live like the Persian *she was not,* the more precarious her position in the court seems to have become. But now that she decides to be the child of God *that she always was;* now that she has resolved to stand *for* her people and let the consequences fall where they may; *now,* having at last determined to risk everything for her people's sake – the crown, her life, everything; *now,* as she comes to the king to plead for her people, *who is it the king sees?* '[T]he king saw *Queen Esther*' (v. 2). And when the king *speaks* to her, who is she? 'What is your wish, *Queen Esther*?' (v. 3).

Gallows Humor (Esther 5) 127

She has, at last, been willing to risk it all. She has laid it all down. She has determined to stand in solidarity with the people of God and the cause of God and the covenant of God and risk her life doing so. But instead of *losing*, she *wins*. Instead of condemnation as a criminal she is recognized as queen. Do you remember Vashti, back in chapter 1? *She* had been queen. But why had *she* been rejected? The king called for her to attend him and she would *not* come. And yet here is Esther, who is ready to lose all by coming without a call, and she is *not* rejected. No, Esther is *recognized* and *received* and promised a *reward*.

Risk met with Reward of Gospel Riches
We've seen in the story so far how Esther has had to make a choice. Would she be the believer or the pagan? The royal consort or the covenant child? Would she risk all or duck and cover? But now the choice is made, and instead of disaster she meets *reward*. And as it turns out, that pattern is not a one-off in scripture. In fact, the same delightful irony laces the promises of the Lord Jesus to all of us who trust Him. You may remember the occasion when Peter reminded Jesus of how much he had sacrificed for His sake. Jesus replied, 'Truly, I say to you, in the new world, when the Son of Man will sit on his glorious throne, you who have followed me will also sit on twelve thrones, judging the twelve tribes of Israel. And everyone who has left houses or brothers or sisters or father or mother or children or lands, for my name's sake, will receive a hundredfold and will inherit eternal life. But many who are first will be last, and the last first' (Matt. 19:28-30).

Esther is a queen, not a criminal. She is rewarded, not condemned. She risks all only to discover that God is no-one's debtor. And *anyone* who ventures to trust in Christ and seek first His kingdom and His righteousness will find all these things added to them also (Matt. 6:33). No-one who has ever given their all for the cause of Christ and in the service of His kingdom will confess to being the loser, however severe the consequences of their faithfulness to Him might have been. With Paul we who have come to know the unsearchable riches of Christ can confess that to us to live is Christ and to die is gain, and as we live and trust in Him, our God supplies all our needs according to His riches in glory.

3. Folly, not Wisdom

Life not death. A queen not a criminal. Then lastly look at verses
9-14. Here is *folly, not wisdom*. Haman is heading home, 'joyful
and glad of heart.' Perhaps he sang a few incoherent songs
as he staggered back from his party with the king. But as
he turned the corner, there was Mordecai in the king's gate,
unafraid, un-trembling, filled with the same serenity that
seems so often to infuriate unbelievers whenever they meet
it in a child of God. And his tipsy good-humors evaporate in
an instant. He is so mad he has to restrain himself, and so, to
self soothe, he calls his friends and family to listen for a while
as he boasted 'of the splendor of his riches, the number of his
sons, all the promotions with which the king had honored
him' (v. 11), advancing him to the top of the civil service
and even including him in the private parties of the royal
family. And yet one thing drives him nuts. 'All this is worth
nothing to me so long as I see Mordecai the Jew sitting at the
king's gate' (v. 13). Enter the most charming character in the
book: Zeresh, Haman's lovely wife. She suggests that a nice
neat hanging ought to relieve poor Haman's stress headache.
Notice the size of the gallows. It is roughly 75 feet tall. Haman
needs gallows to match his ego. Which is exactly the point.

If Esther is the model of wisdom here, Haman is a fool.
His words reveal his folly.[2] And his pride, as towering as
the gallows, can only lead him one way: 'Pride goes before
destruction, and a haughty spirit before a fall' (Prov. 16:18).
The gallows are a monument to Haman's ego. And though
he can't see it, we can: the hint is not hard to catch. For *whom*
is the gallows really intended, in this irony-laden narrative
of sudden reversals? What is the fate of a fool whose biggest
idol is himself?

The joke is really on Haman, and the gallows he has built
to satisfy his bloodlust stands as a warning to us all. While
there is a Savior who has died that we might live, there is a
death that any must face, who, in their foolishness and pride,
reject His offers of mercy. Either *we* die, or *Christ dies for us*.

---

2. Proverbs 13:16: 'In everything the prudent acts with knowledge, but a fool
flaunts his folly.'

6

The Man Whom the King Delights to Honor
(Esther 6)

Reading through the narrative of Esther 6 a phrase from *Hamlet* came to mind. Haman is about to be 'hoist on his own petard'. It's an archaic phrase that we sometimes still hear used to describe a plan that backfires completely. I like words, so I did a little digging to find out its etymology. It turns out that the word *hoist*, as Shakespeare used it, is an archaic past tense. He is not hoist*ed*, but he is *hoist*. And a *petard* was a word of French origin designating a kind of medieval explosive made of gunpowder used by siege engineers to blow open castle doors during a battle. If they set the fuse wrongly, the explosive would go off prematurely and they would be, as Hamlet put it, hoist on their own petard.

In Esther 5, Haman, son of Hammedatha, the Agagite, the enemy of the Jews, has set his (rather short) fuse on an explosion aimed at taking out Mordecai. Having been promoted beyond all others in the kingdom, having had his ego stroked by his inclusion at the private party held by Queen Esther, he has discovered nevertheless that the fragile bubble of success and significance he had so carefully cultivated was easily burst. It was shattered in an instant when his eyes fell on Mordecai, Esther's uncle and adoptive father, bold as brass, unbowed and unafraid, sitting in the king's gate.

Whatever pleasure he had taken from his personal triumphs evaporated in the cruel heat of bitterness and prejudice. And so, at the suggestion of his charming wife, Zeresh, Haman had resolved to deal with Mordecai once and for all. That very night he built enormous gallows, seventy-five feet tall. The next morning he'd go to the king and seek permission to have pesky Mordecai hung on it. The fuse was lit. But Haman, as we'll see, will be hoist on his own petard.

The story is structured around three speeches of King Ahasueras. In verses 1-3, we see the king's insomnia that leads him to ask, 'What honor or distinction has been bestowed on Mordecai…?' The focus here is on *the wisdom of providence*. Then in verses 4-9, the king asks Haman, 'What should be done for the man whom the king delights to honor?' The focus this time is on *the irony of arrogance*. And, finally, in verses 10-13 the king commands Haman to honor Mordecai, so that Haman feels *the sting of vengeance*.

1. The Wisdom of Providence

Understand how high the stakes are as chapter 6 opens. Esther knows only that Haman has secured the king's authorization for the annihilation of the Jews one year on. But she knows nothing of Haman's new resolution to execute Mordecai *that very morning*. In chapters 4 and 5 we watched Esther wrestle with her own responsibility and calling before God. She was called upon to take action and to risk everything. It was a challenging reminder to us all that to follow Christ entails the costliness of faithfulness to His claims in the midst of an increasingly post-Christian world. But now that chapter 6 opens, the focus rests, *not* on *the responsibility of the child of God*, but on *the wise providence of the Sovereign God*. Esther does not even *know* of the fuse that has been lit, moving rapidly towards Mordecai's destruction. It's out of her hands entirely. She can do nothing.

Just as Haman has been up all night building the gallows for Mordecai, so too, it seems, has the king, who does what we've all done when insomnia strikes. He reads. Actually, being the king, he has a talking head read to him. In this case he calls for something called 'the book of memorable deeds, the chronicles.' It was a record of legal decisions, of royal edicts, of battles won, and of tribute paid. It must have been about as riveting a bedtime read as the tax code. One imagines Ahasueras with drooping eyelids and nodding head, about to drift off completely, as the civil servant droned on and on in the background when suddenly the affair of Bigthana[1] and Teresh sends a jolt of electricity through his brain. Mordecai had saved the king's life. But, 'What honor or distinction has been bestowed on Mordecai for this?' (v. 3). The Persian kings were renowned for the extravagant generosity with which they rewarded those who served them well. That Mordecai has gone completely unrewarded was a significant embarrassment that could not go unaddressed. All thought of a good night's sleep was abandoned now. Something had to be done to put things right, and so, 'Who is in the king's court?' (v. 4).

'Now Haman had just entered the outer court of the king's palace to speak to the king about having Mordecai hanged on the gallows that he had prepared for him.' Notice carefully the timing. Ahasueras couldn't sleep. Why? In God's design, he stays up all night in order that he might be reminded of Mordecai's heroism in saving his life. When he sent to the palace for an advisor to rectify the situation, who should be walking in the door but Haman, who's at the palace unusually early, presumably because he couldn't wait any longer to tell the king of his plan for Mordecai. God has set up Ahasueras and Haman, do you see, timing everything perfectly, that the blood lust of the latter might be undone by the guilt of the former, for the salvation of His own beloved child.

Here is the wisdom of providence on display. It is a beautiful reminder to us that 'The heart of man plans his way, but the LORD establishes his steps' (Prov. 16:9). It is a reminder to us that God does indeed work 'all things according to the counsel of his own will' (Eph. 1:11). It is a reminder that 'God works all things together for the good of those who love him and are called according to his purpose' (Rom. 8:28).

Esther 6 helps us to fight anxiety with faith in the wise providence of God. Queen Esther was ignorant of the situation and so quite impotent to help. Mordecai was in danger, his

---

1. Bigthana is an alternative spelling of Bigthan (see Esther 2:21).

life threatened. If Haman had persuaded Ahasueras to order the annihilation of the Jewish people so simply, how hard will it be for him to secure one man's execution? Humanly speaking it was a terrifying turn of events. But, Esther 6:1, 'On that night, *that very night*, the king could not sleep.' God was at work for the good of Mordecai in ways beyond understanding. The malice of Haman and the vacuous, amoral, hedonism of Ahasueras presented no barrier to the Lordship of the God of heaven.

Have you perhaps forgotten that word of Christ which says, 'Which of you by being anxious can add a single hour to his span of life?... Do not be anxious about tomorrow, for tomorrow will be anxious for itself. Sufficient for the day is its own trouble' (Matt. 6:27, 34). Do you live in the grip of worry about forces beyond your control? Our *fear* is an excellent barometer of how far we continue to misunderstand the true dynamics that govern all things. Our worry derives from the belief that we *ought* to be competent for every circumstance while discovering that in fact we are not. Maybe you have been living out this equation over and over again: *unforeseeable circumstances, plus misplaced faith in your own competence, has equaled anxiety and fear*. But the word of the Lord in Esther 6 calls us to direct our confidence to a far more reliable object than *ourselves*, it invites us to lift our eyes to the hills and to remember from whence our help comes. Our safety comes from the Lord, the maker of heaven and earth (Ps. 121:2). It aims to help us rejoin the Psalmist in singing with renewed confidence in the only solid foundation for faith: 'Some trust in chariots and some in horses, *but we trust in the name of the* LORD *our God*' (Ps. 20:7).

A Pattern of Provision

Of course, this pattern of God's wise and gracious provision for His people before even they knew how much they needed it is never more clearly seen than at the Cross. 'For while we were still weak, at the right time Christ died for the ungodly... while we were still sinners, Christ died for us... while we were enemies we were reconciled to God by the death of his Son' (Rom. 5:6, 8, 10). Still sinners, still ungodly, still weak, still enemies... ignorant of grace, self-reliant, proud, rebels. That is who we were. And while we were helpless and headed for destruction, like Mordecai in face of Haman's plot, God nevertheless acted for us in mercy and grace, and by the Cross of His Son, obtained for us salvation.

We may believe in the Gospel and trust in Christ crucified, but we give the lie to that profession when we give in to fear about our future. The God who acted by His Son to save us while we were still sinners, acts in countless ways beyond our ken, to guard us and keep us and bring us home to glory remade in the image of His Son at the last.

2. The Irony of Arrogance

In verses 4-9, Haman is found standing in the outer court and is immediately ushered into the king's presence. Very quickly things move from the sublime to the slapstick. It is difficult not to laugh out loud as Ahasueras asks his question, 'What shall be done to the man whom the king delights to honor?' (v. 6). And Haman said to himself, 'Whom would the king delight to honor more than me?'

It's the first time in the story we are told what someone is *thinking*. Literally we are told, 'Haman said *in his heart*, "Whom would the king delight to honor more than me?"' We are being shown *the heart of Haman*. To no-one's surprise, we find that it is *Haman* that has first place in Haman's heart. He can think of no one better suited to reward than himself. In his reply, none of the customary courtly niceties, so much in evidence in Esther's dealing with the king in chapter 5, are to be found. There is no, 'If it pleases the king...' (5:4); no 'If I have found favor in your eyes....' (5:8). Haman is *so* eager for the plaudits of the king that he rushes right in, all the pleasantries forgotten, like a kid at Christmas who grabs the gift with hungry eyes and nary a thank you. Look at verses 8-9. Haman wants the king's own robes and the king's own horse, and a ticker-tape parade through the city streets. Some commentators suggest that Haman was in effect asking to be proclaimed the king's equal, or at least his surrogate, or heir. Here's a window into Haman's heart. We get to see the nature of the man as clearly as ever we have, and we are being invited to laugh out loud at the sheer folly of what we find.

Haman has made an idol of *himself*, and his *ego* has made a fool of *him*. All the while Haman is telling the king what he wants for himself, the king only hears good advice on how best to honor the one man that Haman wants to destroy. The exquisite comedy of the narrative is crowned by the punch-line in verse 10: 'Hurry, take the robes and the horse as you have said and do so to... *Mordecai the Jew,* who sits at the king's gate. Leave out nothing you have mentioned.' The blood drains from Haman's face. He has been caught in his own trap. He has been hoist on his own petard.

Laughing at the Ludicrous

It's a Psalm 2 moment. 'The kings of the earth set themselves, and the rulers take counsel together, against the LORD and against his Anointed, saying, "Let us burst their bonds apart and cast away their cords from us." He who sits in the heavens laughs; the Lord holds them in derision' (Ps. 2:2-4). Haman's arrogance has made him a joke at whom even the Lord Himself laughs and holds him in derision. There is a solemn warning there for us about the futility and emptiness of pursuing earthly glory. Psalm 115:8 says of those who run after idols: 'Those who make them become like them; so do all who trust in them.' The folly of idolatry, the thing that makes it so ludicrous and ultimately laughable, is that, instead of our idols of money and power and influence and ease beautifying us, they leave us as empty as they are. Those who make idols become like them – as dumb as a block of wood, as shiny as gold, and just as lifeless.

Be warned by Haman's folly and hear with new ears the call of Psalm 2: 'Now therefore, O kings, be wise; be warned, O rulers of the earth. Serve the LORD with fear and rejoice with trembling. Kiss the Son, lest he be angry, and you perish in the way, for his wrath is quickly kindled. Blessed are all who take refuge in him' (Ps. 2:10-12). It is not in finding a way to be exalted above all others that we find peace and blessing but only in bowing before the exalted Son, the Lord Jesus Christ, and fleeing to take refuge in Him.

3. The Sting of Vengeance

In verses 10-13, the king orders Haman to do for Mordecai what he longed for himself: the robe, the horse, the procession, all of it. One wonders what Mordecai must have been thinking that morning when Haman came stomping up to him with his face like a thundercloud, an army of civil servants in tow. And the bewilderment when instead of the violence Haman's dirty looks seemed to promise, Haman has the sackcloth with which Mordecai was dressed replaced with the royal robes of the king, mounts him on the king's own horse, and then walks ahead of him shouting to all how great a guy Mordecai is and how much the king delights to honor him.

By the end of the day Mordecai – faithful Mordecai, reliable Mordecai, was back where he always is – in the king's gate, while Haman was home sulking. Notice the stunning reversal. Mordecai is dressed like a king and is serving at the palace. Haman heads for home mourning – the word is the same as the mourning the Jews engaged in when Haman's edicts for their destruction was first announced in 4:1 and 3. Haman and Mordecai have traded places. And just when things could not get any darker for Haman, cue Zeresh, as delightful as ever, with words of cold comfort. When she heard from Haman all that had occurred she said, 'If Mordecai before whom you have begun to fall is of the Jewish people, you will not overcome him but will surely fall before him.'

How are Zeresh and her cronies able to make that determination? It is not at all clear, though it seems likely that even they are beginning to discern something of the providential care of God for His chosen people. The language they use calls Mordecai, literally, 'the seed of the Jews', which to them meant nothing, but to us as readers of the whole Bible, it's a title that rings with promise. Remember that what we are seeing played out here is another iteration of the age-old conflict between the Benjamites and the Agagites, between Israel and her enemies, between the church and the world, between the Seed of the Woman and the seed of the Serpent. Mordecai is the seed of Abraham to whom belong the covenant promises. And though Zeresh may not have been able to account for all her reasoning, she says more than she knows when she tells Haman that against the covenant seed there can be no victory.

It had been four years that Mordecai had gone forgotten and unrewarded. During that time the fate of the people of

God in the empire had gone from bad to worse. But God has not forgotten His covenant, and in His own perfect timing He works to keep His promises.

A Chilling Warning and A Covenant Promise
Earlier we quoted Psalm 115:8 as a good description of the fate of Haman: 'those who make idols become like them, so do all who trust in them.' In that same psalm, the idolatrous nations are quoted as asking of Israel, 'Where now is their God?' If we are not believers, there is a temptation to think ourselves safe because we cannot see God at work or discern His ways. We may scoff and mock the people of God for their convictions and their ethics. And for the church the temptation to begin to wonder if God has in fact forgotten His promises to His people can be just as real. We find ourselves asking, 'Where is the promise of his coming? For ever since the fathers fell asleep, all things are continuing as they were from the beginning of creation' (2 Pet. 3:4). Or we begin to cry out with the psalmist, 'How long, O Lord?'

But, if we are not Christians, Esther 6 is a chilling warning. And if we are, it is a glorious promise of hope. It tells us that God 'is not slow in keeping his promise as some account slowness, but is patient toward you, not wishing that any should perish, but that all should reach repentance. But the day of the Lord will come like a thief, and then the heavens will pass away with a roar, and the heavenly bodies will be burned up and dissolved, and the earth and the works that are done on it will be exposed' (2 Pet. 3:9-10).

An echo of that great final day reached Haman in the words of Zeresh his wife. God will and does keep covenant with His people, however long He might delay. If you are not a Christian, be warned. Repent and believe the gospel, lest a sudden reversal come upon you like a thief in the night and you feel the sting of divine vengeance. But if you are a Christian, endure, press on; learn from Mordecai, what the man whom the *Lord* delights to honor is like, and like him, do not grow weary in well doing, knowing that we shall reap a harvest in due time if we do not give up.

7

The Big Reveal
(Esther 6:14–7:10)

As human beings we are living in the grip of a terrible dilemma. It's what we'll call 'the problem of God'. Our problem is not really with what the Bible calls sin. We do not have a sin problem. We love sin. Sin is comfortable and easy, and it comes naturally. Who has a problem with sin? No, our problem lies elsewhere. We do not have a sin problem. We have a God problem. God is a problem for sinners because they love their sin *and He does not.* While we excuse our sin and justify our sin and minimize our sin and blame others for our sin, God never lets us off the hook. God is holy. We are not. The deepest problem of the human condition, of your heart and my heart, is a God problem

Some of you may know what I'm talking about. You are sleeping with someone you shouldn't. You are watching something you shouldn't. You are lying about your finances because your spending is out of control and you're ashamed. You nurse bitterness and you will not let the simmering resentment go, and years have passed since the original injury, but your pride keeps it all alive. But God demands moral change of you. And so your conscience sears and stings. But you don't change. You don't stop the affair, or the porn, or the spending, or the rage. You *love* your sin. No, you have a *God* problem, not a sin problem. In fact, our God problem is much worse than we realize. The Bible teaches us that if our sin is not dealt with, our God problem will not simply sting our consciences. It will condemn us forever. We have a God problem of *cosmic* proportions.

But what if I told you that the God whose holiness stings our consciences does far more than simply demand moral reformation? What if I were to tell you that though God does indeed claim the total allegiance of your heart and the complete forsaking of your pet sin, He does not stand off, away at a distance, with arms folded as it were, waiting to see if you will meet His standards? What if the God of infinite purity, whose glory is inimical to sin, hostile to it, is nevertheless turned towards you as a sinner in infinite love? What if all the initiative, all the work in overcoming our God problem, was borne by God Himself? Wouldn't you begin to think about the deepest issues of your heart in a new way? Wouldn't it change everything? As we consider Esther 7 we are going to see two principles which, if we embrace them, will do exactly that.

1. The Principle of Identification
Let's look at 6:14–7:6 first. Haman has just had the worst bad-hair day of his life. He has been promoted to the No. 2 spot in the kingdom. He has been included in the royal family's private parties. He has set in motion a plan to eradicate the Jews, whom he hates, and he has built gallows 75 feet tall on which to hang Mordecai, the object of his racism and loathing. Everything had been going swimmingly for Haman until his early morning visit to the palace earlier that day. No sooner had he arrived than he found himself ushered into the king's presence and quizzed about how best to honor a man upon whom the special favor of Ahasueras had fallen. Naturally, Haman, whose ego was so swollen it had blotted out all sight of anyone or anything but himself, thought the king was planning to honor him. Instead, as he found to his dismay, the man whom the king delights to honor was Mordecai, and Haman, to his utter humiliation, was required both to facilitate and to publicly herald Mordecai's reward.

We left Haman in the sour company of what people from my home town in Scotland would have called his 'nippy wee wife' Zeresh who appears to be full of nothing but poison.

She was quick to suggest, remember, Mordecai's murder, and equally quick to predict her husband's doom too: 'If Mordecai, before whom you have begun to fall, is of the seed of the Jews, you will not overcome him but will surely fall before him.' What a sweetheart. Haman is having a really bad day. Things have spiraled rapidly out of his control. His plans have begun to unravel in a most disturbing way. And verse 14 is meant to convey something of that. 'While they were yet talking with him, the king's eunuchs arrived and hurried to bring Haman to the feast that Esther had prepared.' In other words, Haman wasn't ready. His master plan has begun to fall apart, and his life is spinning out of control. He's wallowing in misery with Zeresh and her cronies when the eunuchs come and hurry him to the feast. One almost gets the sense of Haman being whisked away, mid-sentence, utterly discombobulated, his mouth hanging open, spluttering his outrage.

Sudden Reversals, yet Again
In the opening sections of the book it was *Esther*, Hadassah, the pretty Jewish peasant girl, who had been swept away by palace eunuchs to an uncertain fate. It was *Esther* whose life had been disrupted by plans not her own. But now, as Haman and Ahasueras sit down at Esther's third banquet, Queen Esther presides, and *Haman* is the one who is swept along, out of control, and overtaken by circumstances that were never part of his plan. We are being reminded, yet again, that our ways are not God's ways, nor are our thoughts God's thoughts (Isa. 55:8). His ends and designs are subtler and wiser than any plan of ours, and whatever our plots and schemes may intend, 'God works all things according to the counsel of his own will' (Eph. 1:11). He 'treasures up his strange designs and works his sovereign will'.[1]

And so now the wine is flowing as Esther's third banquet draws to a close. We imagine Haman, beginning to relax after his earlier humiliation in the king's palace. 'After all,' he might have told himself. 'Things are not so bad. My plan is not a total loss. The Jews remain under a death sentence.' But if Haman was left to muse distractedly on his stinging reversals,

---

1. William Cowper, *God Moves in a Mysterious Way*.

Ahasueras has only one thing on his mind. He was pressing his desire to *finally* get to the bottom of Esther's request. This is now the third time he has asked her to tell him why she had risked her neck to visit him without an invitation. It is the third time he had publicly, and extravagantly, promised her anything she wished, up to half his kingdom. Esther has pushed this dangerously unstable and capricious tyrant to the brink, and the time now has come at last for 'the big reveal'.

Notice her judicious reply. 'If I have found favor in your sight, O king, and if it please the king, let my life be granted to me for my *wish*, and my people for my *request*. For we have been sold, I and my people' (v. 3). Note that: 'we have been sold' – probably an oblique reference to the money Haman had offered to pay into the treasury to cover the costs of his holocaust. And then she quotes the edict against her people verbatim. In all likelihood, self-absorbed Ahasueras is oblivious to the specific law she is talking about. No, this is for Haman's benefit. 'We have been sold, I and my people, to be destroyed, to be killed, and to be annihilated.' Haman has just spilled his wine all down his already disheveled robes. The queen, *the queen,* is Jewish. Haman's bad-hair day just got a whole lot worse.

Wisdom at Work

Then Esther appeals to the king's self-interest, but not without some honest autobiography thrown in to lend pathos to her point. Look at verse 4: 'If we had been sold merely as slaves, men and women, I would have been silent, for our affliction is not to be compared with the loss to the king.' Esther herself, remember, had been all but enslaved as a sex object in the harem of the king. She knows whereof she speaks. In fact, if it was merely a matter of harsh treatment, hadn't that been the lot of the Jewish people since entering exile? 'But that's not what *this* is, King Ahasueras. No, this will directly affect your revenues throughout the empire. What a loss to the king if the Jews are to be destroyed.'

She knows exactly which buttons to press. It's the perfect mix of deference and forthrightness, cunning and simplicity. Esther has become a master politician, skilled at speaking truth to power, and we cannot help but admire the poise and courage with which she has learned to play and win the deadly games of Persian court life. She is as wise as a serpent and as gentle as a dove, the very embodiment and personification of Lady Wisdom from Proverbs 8.

And as the king bristles in outrage at Esther's revelation – 'Who is he, and where is he who has dared to do this?' – Esther knows that the time for subtlety and cunning is finally past. The time for being coy is over. Now is the moment to strike. Verse 5 really must be read with a shout of victory. All the niceties of courtly manners, so much a part of all her addresses to the king until now, give way before the torrent of raw emotion that is packed into this climactic line. 'A foe and an enemy. This wicked Haman.' The trap *snaps* shut and Haman was caught. He was, we are told, terrified before the king and the queen.

It was a master-stroke. But it was also an incredibly risky move. You see what Esther has done? She has revealed, not just her long overdue request to the king, but *she has also revealed her long hidden identity to Haman*, her mortal enemy. In order to secure her people's salvation she must risk her own destruction. Even more than that, in order for Esther to be saved herself, she must identify with the very people who have been condemned to die.

A Stunning Picture of a Yet-Sweeter Gospel

And as we watch her courage and self-sacrifice, as we trace out that pattern of selfless solidarity with those under the sentence of death, are not our eyes directed beyond her to Another, into whose likeness we have watched her become increasingly transformed? Again and again, and with growing clarity as her duty became clear to her, Esther has pointed us, like a flashing neon arrow, away from herself, to the Lord Jesus Christ. And never has she done so more clearly than here. In order to secure the salvation of her people she must be *identified* with a people who stand under a sentence of death. The law of the king has proclaimed their destruction. But Esther stands in solidarity with them. She is identified with them. She becomes one of them, placing herself under their sentence. And as she does so, she secures their redemption.

There is an echo there, isn't there, clear and strong, of the gospel of Jesus Christ? But the truth is, the gospel is so much sweeter. *Esther* secures only *temporal* deliverance from the unjust tyranny of an *earthly* monarch. *Jesus* secures *eternal salvation* from the *just and holy judgment of Almighty God*. *Esther* stands with her people and intercedes on their behalf. *Jesus* stands with His people *and dies in their place*. *Esther* must persuade the king to spare the Jews. But in *Jesus*, the God whose law condemns us, *Himself bears its penalty and secures our pardon*.

It's the principle of identification. The moving commitment of Esther to her people, pales before the wonderful gospel of grace in which God, in Christ, identifies with sinners. That statement alone will fuel an eternity's praise. God, in Christ, identifies with sinners. He does not stand afar off, with arms folded, as it were, to see if we will meet His moral standards. No, He comes to us in Jesus; all the way down to us, in Jesus, as one of us, 'born of a woman, born under the law, to redeem those under the Law' (Gal. 4:4). God was, in Christ, reconciling the world to Himself (2 Cor. 5:19).

2. The Principle of Propitiation   *To satisfy the wrath of God against sin*

But there is another principle in Esther 7. Not just the principle of identification, but *the principle of propitiation*. You can see it in action in verses 7-10.

The king arose in his wrath from the wine drinking (v. 7) and went into the palace garden. Now, why did he do that? Was he so out of control that he needed to step outside for some air? Perhaps. More likely, the king was fretting over the extravagant and very public promises he had made to Esther: he would give her whatever she asked for, up to half his kingdom. But what she wants, he now realizes, is the reversal of a royal decree delegated to Haman. He has publicly bound himself to do Esther's bidding, but he'd also publicly delegated authority to Haman. He could not accede to Esther's request without humiliating himself in compromising his decisions with respect to Haman's leadership. Ahasueras was stuck. What to do? To paraphrase that great repository of theological wisdom, *The Sound of Music*, the problem facing Ahasueras was, 'How do you solve a problem like Haman?'

Meanwhile, Haman did something that he must have known was against the law. In the Persian court, a man was forbidden from being left alone with a member of the king's harem, and even in the presence of the king no-one was permitted within seven steps of one of the royal concubines. But Haman, the highest civil servant in the empire, is so distraught at the doom he sees opening before him, ready to swallow him whole, that all sense of what is and is not lawful in the king's court is forgotten. He throws himself on Esther's mercy, literally falling onto the couch upon which she is seated, just as the king re-enters the room.

Ahasueras takes the scene in at a glance and realizes that Haman had just handed him a convenient resolution to his dilemma. 'Will he even assault the queen in my presence, in my own house?' (v. 8). He is not really serious in suggesting that Haman was attempting to rape the queen. But his proximity to her person was close enough to make the charges stick. Now he could dispatch Haman, save the queen, reverse his edict and not lose face.

While his attendants put a black bag over Haman's head, Harbona (v. 9) has a brain wave: 'You know, there is this gallows, all shiny and new, in Haman's back yard…. It was meant for Mordecai, whose word saved the king.' 'Perfect. Hang him on that.'

And as Haman is dispatched, look at the end of verse 10: 'The wrath of the king abated.' More than that, with Haman's death the law is satisfied, the demands of justice met, and the security of the Jews put beyond all doubt. As long as Haman lived, there was no way for the king to meet Esther's wish without losing face. As long as Haman lived, the offense against the king remained. As long as Haman lived, the Jewish people faced a sentence of death. But when Haman died, the wrath of the king abated and the people were saved.

That is the principle of *propitiation*. Propitiation means the satisfaction of wrath by means of sacrifice. The death of Haman propitiated the wrath of the king. 'The wrath of the king abated.' Propitiation. It's a principle that stands at the very heart of the gospel. We said earlier that the Lord Jesus identified with His people. He stood with us under our sentence of death, in solidarity with us, that He might deliver us. But the question remains, how exactly did that act of solidarity and identification obtain our rescue? And the answer is *propitiation*.

Roles Reversed
Now in our story it is the *enemy* of God's people, the opponent of the cause and covenant of God, that dies to satisfy wrath. It's Haman. But in the gospel, it is not the enemy that dies. That's *us*. We have met the enemy, and he is us. We are the enemy. We are all Haman in this tale – by nature rebels against God. No, in the gospel it's not the enemy that dies. In the gospel, the one who dies to satisfy wrath *is* the one whose wrath has been kindled against us. The gospel is that it is God Himself who bears the penalty and pays the price. God made Jesus who knew no sin to be sin for us (2 Cor. 5:21). God was in Christ reconciling the world to Himself (2 Cor. 5:19).

'In this is love,' John says, 'not that we have loved God but that he loved us and sent his Son to be the propitiation for our sins' (1 John 4:10). This is the love of God at its fullest demonstration: the One whose law condemns us, *takes flesh and pays the debt for us, bears the sanctions for us, bears the curse for us.* Unlike the Esther story, where Haman is made the propitiatory scapegoat, the wonder of the gospel, the thing that makes the apostle John sing in wonder at God's love, is that *God* propitiates *Himself*, in Christ, for us.

A God Problem and a Gospel Solution
Now, go back with me to our God problem, for a minute. By nature, we don't have a sin problem – we *like* our sin – we have a *God* problem. But when we come to realize what God has done for us, in His marvelous love – when we come to see that the God who condemns our sin utterly, has come all the way down to us in Christ, identifying with us, standing in solidarity with us, and dies for us to satisfy the condemnation our sin deserves – when we grasp *that*, doesn't that change everything? People who grasp that, and are gripped by that, no longer think as they once did. Instead of loving their sin but struggling with a God problem, what happens? Instead of loving their sin and struggling with a God problem, *now*, because of the gospel, *they love God and only struggle with a sin*

problem. That is the nature of Christian conversion. When the glory and grace of the gospel illuminates our natural darkness, we move from loving sin and struggling with a God problem, to loving God, because of Jesus, and struggling with a sin problem. Because of Jesus, the God who *was* a condemnatory judge, from whom we once ran, makes Himself Abba Father, into whose arms we joyfully flee.

Which best describes you? Do you love sin and wrestle with a God problem? Do you live with the sting of a condemning conscience, knowing you live a life of rebellion? Understand if you do, that one day, unless you can be reconciled to God, the sting of a condemning conscience will be replaced for you by an eternal condemnation from which there will be no escape. But understand too, that *that need not be the fate of anyone.* God was in Christ reconciling the world to Himself (2 Cor. 5:19). This is love, not that we have loved God but that He loved us and sent His Son to be the propitiation for our sins (1 John 4:10). Everything has been done to deal with your God-problem once and for all. All you need do is trust in the Lord Jesus Christ.

8

Eucatastrophe
(Esther 8)

On 7th November 1944, the author of *The Hobbit* and *The Lord of The Rings,* J. R. R. Tolkien, penned a letter to his son Christopher in which he defined a word of his own invention that stood at the heart of his vision of what makes a story, especially fairy stories, truly great. He called it *eucatastrophe* – a good catastrophe. 'I coined the word "eucatastrophe",' he said. It means 'the sudden happy turn in a story which pierces you with a joy that brings tears'. He likened the sudden relief that *eucatastrophe* brings to the snapping back into place of a limb that had been put out of joint. … Joyous relief.[1]

The Book of Esther, from chapter 8 on to the end of the story, is a *eucatastrophe*. Remember, everything had been going wrong for Esther and Mordecai and the people of God in exile in the Persian Empire. But in chapter 7 the first rays of a new sunrise had begun to crest the horizon. Haman was 'hoist on his own petard', caught in his own trap, quite literally hung on his own gallows. But Ahasueras, the Persian Emperor, had permitted Haman to pronounce an edict declaring the universal destruction of the Jewish people and, Haman's death notwithstanding, that decree still stood. And Esther 8 shows us how the great reversal, the *eucatastrophe*

---

1. J. R. R. Tolkien. *The Letters of J. R. R. Tolkien* (London: Harper Collins, 2012), Letter 89.

in this story, actually comes about by which those who were doomed to die were delivered and made to conquer.

There are four things to consider in this passage. First, in verses 1-2, there is *the reward*; second, in verses 3-8, there is *the request*; third, in 9-14, there is *the reversal*; and fourth, in 15-17, there is *the rejoicing*.

1. The Reward (8:1-2)

Haman has met his untimely end on that state-of-the-art, best-that-money-can-buy, macabre Persian status symbol: the shiny new seventy-five-foot-tall gallows he had built and intended for his archenemy, Mordecai. But Esther had sprung her trap with consummate skill. Ahasueras could not resist her wiles, and Haman could not escape her revenge. He has been dragged from the king's presence with a black bag over his head, taken away to face justice. And now chapter 8 opens later that same day, in the palace. And as the dust settles, notice what the king does.

He bestows Haman's house – his estates and possessions – upon Queen Esther, and then 'Mordecai came before the king, for Esther had told what he was to her. And the king' – listen to this; how's this for a great reversal? – 'And the king took off his signet ring, which he had taken from Haman, and gave it Mordecai. And Esther set Mordecai over the house of Haman.'

Mordecai replaces Haman as the king's right-hand man, No. 2 in the empire, and he rules from the very home that once belonged to his enemy. From rags to riches, from death to life, from the ashes of mourning to the palace of royal glory. That's the trajectory of the story. And it is a trajectory we find repeated in Scripture, and one that will eventually sweep up into it the people of God as a whole. Mordecai and Esther are but two more in the long line of righteous sufferers whom God will reward in the end. One thinks of the Song of Hannah where, reflecting on God's intervention amidst her own sorrows, she said of her situation in 1 Samuel 2:6-8: 'The Lord kills and brings to life; he brings down to Sheol and raises up. The Lord makes poor and makes rich; he brings low and he exalts. *He raises up the poor from the dust; he lifts the needy from the ash heap to make them sit with princes and inherit a seat of honor.*'

Isn't that exactly what has happened here? God has taken vulnerable Esther, and Mordecai – derelict, and bereft of power, literally sitting in ashes, mourning outside the king's gate – and has brought them to life and raised them up to the sit with princes and inherit a seat of honor. It's Proverbs 11:8 in action: 'The righteous is delivered from trouble, and the wicked walks into it instead.' *Righteousness is always worthwhile, but sin is ultimately self-defeating.* That is the point.

From Trial to Triumph: The Pattern of Christ
We are being helped here to endure our own privations and trials for the Lord's sake. We are to endure hardship, and not to lose heart, nor be surprised at the fiery trials that come upon us (1 Pet. 4:12). We are to be ready to sit in the ashes, as *Hannah's* prayer put it, and to suffer for being a Christian and not be ashamed, but to glorify God as the *Apostle Peter* put it in 1 Peter 4:16, knowing that if we will 'not grow weary of going good… in due season we will reap, if we do not give up', as the *Apostle Paul* put it (Gal. 6:9). And we are to do it, of course, because this is a pattern set for us, not simply by a long line of scriptural heroes and heroines like Hannah and Esther and Mordecai and Job and David and Jeremiah and Daniel. We are to do it because it is a pattern that finds its *climactic expression* in the patient, selfless suffering and glorious, exalted reward of the Lord Jesus Christ Himself.

That is Paul's point in Philippians 2. As believers we are to 'have the same mind among ourselves, which is ours in Christ, who, though he was in the form of God, did not count equality with God a thing to be grasped, but *emptied* himself, by taking the form of a *servant*, being born in the likeness of men. And being found in human form, he *humbled* himself by becoming obedient to the point of death, even death on a cross' (Phil. 2:5-8). Here is Christ Himself, the Lord of glory, sitting, as Hannah said, in the ashes of humiliation, in the dust of obedience and death, for us and for our salvation. Here He is, who, 'though he was rich, yet he became poor,' that we might become rich (2 Cor. 8:9). But it didn't end there in the ashes of suffering. The joy that followed sorrow for Hanna and Esther and Mordecai was but a pale shadow of the glorious reality of God's final response to the trials of this world. Considering that he has borne our sorrows and paid for our sins, Paul goes on to say, '*Therefore* God has highly exalted him and bestowed on him the name that is above every name, so that at the name of Jesus every knee should bow, in heaven and on earth and under the earth, and every tongue confess that Jesus Christ is Lord, to the glory of God the Father' (Phil. 2:9-10).

Isn't that ultimately what is going on here? Mordecai's elevation from the dust of mourning to the seat of power is a reminder of God's promise to all His suffering children that God is no man's debtor; that 'the righteous is delivered from trouble, and the wicked walks into it instead'; that righteousness is always worthwhile, but sin is ultimately self-defeating; that, if we will 'not grow weary of going good… in due season we will reap, if we do not give up' (Gal. 6:9). And it is a reminder, *supremely*, that this is the pattern into which Christ Himself entered, not only as our example, but also as our redeemer. The joy into which *He* was brought in glory is the guarantee of *ours*, who love and follow Him. Therefore, let us bear our trials with patience, knowing the reward that God has promised.

2. The Request (8:3-8)

Esther and Mordecai may be personally secure now in the king's good graces, but the edict against the Jewish people still remains. And so, for the second time in the narrative, Esther drops her guard. The first time was when, with a shout of victory, she denounced Haman before the king: 'A foe and an enemy. This wicked Haman.' And now her emotions overtake her once again, but they are no longer feelings of jubilation and triumph, but overwhelming sorrow and urgent concern on behalf of her people. 'She fell at his feet and wept and pleaded with him to avert the evil plan of Haman the Agagite' (v. 3). No doubt all the tension of the days leading up to the confrontation with Haman at last overtakes her; all the raw emotion, held in check for so long, comes pouring out, as she desperately intercedes on her people's behalf.

As the king holds out the golden scepter to her, giving her permission to speak – and time to compose herself too – Esther at last manages to articulate her request with some semblance of courtly propriety. Nevertheless, the urgency and intensity still cannot be hidden. 'Esther rose and stood before the king. And she said, "If it please the king, and if I have found favor in his sight, and if the thing seems right before the king, and I am pleasing in his eyes, let an order be written to revoke the letters devised by Haman the Agagite, the son of Hammedatha, which he wrote to destroy the Jews who are in all the provinces of the king. For how can I *bear* to see the calamity that is coming to my people? Or how can I *bear* to see the destruction of my kindred?"' (Esther 8:5-6).

Importunate, Prayerful Pleading
The word used of Esther's pleading in verse 3 has the sense of urgent, desperate intercession. An old word *importunity* captures the meaning well: insistent, bold, self-forgetful, shameless pleading. It's the word used in Jesus' parable, illustrating persistent prayer, in Luke 11:8. A friend comes at midnight asking for bread for a guest who has arrived unexpectedly. The answer comes down, 'Do not bother me; the door is now shut, and my children are with me in bed. I cannot get up and give you anything.' And Jesus concludes, 'I tell you, though he will not get up and give him anything because he is his friend, yet because of his importunity, his insistence, his urgent pleading, he will rise and give him whatever he needs.'

If the importunate pleadings of the neighbor seeking bread in Jesus' parable, and Esther's importunate pleadings for temporal deliverance for her people from a wicked tyrant, if *they* obtained their desired results, *Jesus'* point in Luke 11 is, how much more ready ought *we* to be, as the children of God, *to plead importunately with our Father in heaven*, to ask and to seek and to knock, knowing that unlike the sleepy neighbor in Jesus' story, or the wicked king in Esther's life, *our Father in heaven stands ready to give good gifts to those who ask Him* (Matt. 7:11).

God *has* promised us that the sufferings of this present time are not worth comparing to the glory that is to be revealed to us (Rom. 8:18). *But He has also ordained that the pathway through the sufferings of this present time, to the glory to be revealed, is the pathway of faithful, importunate prayer.* What right have we to expect a place in the coming kingdom, if we never pray with urgency and devotion, 'Your kingdom come, your will be done on earth as it is in heaven' (Matt. 6:10)?

3. The Reversal (8:9-14)

Esther has poured out her request, and the king, for his part, reassures Esther, that she and Mordecai are now in fact in a position *themselves* to undo the edict Haman had enacted. Mordecai now wears the royal signet ring and rules as vizier and second in command. Oh, it's true, Persian laws could not be revoked exactly, but they *could* be contradicted. They *could* be countermanded. A new law *could* supersede the old: 'Use the authority that comes with your new office, Mordecai, and secure your people's deliverance.'

And so, the scribes are summoned. An edict is written and sent to all the satraps and governors and the officials of the provinces from India to Ethiopia, all 127 provinces, in each language. It is sent using the vast and efficient Persian courier network, on the fastest horses available. *Now* it is the *Jews* who are to defend themselves against the aggressors who will attempt to enforce Haman's original decree. *Now* it is the *Jews* who are to 'destroy, to kill, and to annihilate' any armed force that might attack them. They are to destroy their enemy's lives and families and plunder their goods '*on a single day, the thirteenth day of the month of Adar*' (v. 12).

Eucatastrophe: A Sudden Reversal of the Enemy's Plan
Did you hear the echo there of Haman's original decree, back in chapter 3? The mention of the scribes, the provincial government officials, the language of 'destroy, kill, annihilate', the appointment of the thirteenth day of Adar, the couriers used to deliver the message – the author of the book is careful to show us that in Mordecai's new edict we have a blow by blow undoing of Haman's original decree. It is a *eucatastrophe*. It is the sudden reversal of the enemy's plan, snatching triumph from the jaws of defeat. It is death swallowed up in victory (1 Cor. 15:54).

When Tolkien coined the term *eucatastrophe,* this idea of sudden and happy reversal, of evil undone, he said it made for such great storytelling because 'it is a sudden glimpse of Truth... It perceives ... that this is indeed how things really do work in the Great World[2] for which our nature is made. And I concluded by saying that the Resurrection was the greatest "eucatastrophe" possible... and produces that essential emotion: Christian joy.'[3]

That's exactly right. Here, in the *eucatastrophe* that broke in upon Esther and her people during the reign of Ahasueras of Persia, is an adumbration, an anticipation and echo, a foretaste and preview of the greatest *eucatastrophe* of all, when death itself was undone: and Satan in all his malice was at last defeated, and the grave's power was broken, and Christ rose in triumph. Esther's tale is a tale of a great reversal. But it ought to remind us of the greatest reversal of all, when our Redeemer made satisfaction for sins, and overcame death, and rose in glory. And it invites us to wait for the day when we ourselves shall be swept up into participation in Christ's victory, in a *eucatastrophe* of our own. One day the trumpet of the archangel shall sound, and Christ shall split the sky, coming in glory with His angels, and every eye shall see Him (Rev. 1:7; Luke 21:27), and we who believe shall all be changed, and the dead shall rise (1 Cor. 15:51-52), and the heavens will be rolled up like a scroll (Rev. 6:14; Isa. 34:4), and the elements melt as in a fire (2 Pet. 3:10-12). The books will be opened (Rev. 21:27) and all the enemies of Christ and His Church will be destroyed (Rev. 21:7-8), and a new heaven and a new earth will open to us (Rev. 21:1), the home of righteousness where we shall be forever with the Lord, face to face (Rev. 22:4; 1 Cor. 13:12), as the Lamb wipes away every tear from our eyes (Rev. 21:4).

4. The Rejoicing (8:15-17)

Tolkien said that 'the Resurrection was the greatest "eucatastrophe" possible... and produces that essential emotion: *Christian joy*.' Part of the reversal of Esther's story is this: Haman's original edict to destroy the Jews had thrown Susa, the capitol, into confusion and uproar, and had brought the Jews into mourning and fasting and grief.

---

2. By 'the Great World' here, Tolkien is referring to heaven.

3. Tolkien, *Letters*, Letter 89.

Notice then, in verses 16 and 17, that the *fasting* is replaced with *feasting*, the *mourning* is replaced with *rejoicing*, and the *grief* is replaced with *gladness*. Those who once distanced themselves from a people marked for destruction, now join them – declaring themselves Jews, 'for fear of the Jews had fallen on them.' And yet, as wonderful as the celebration no doubt was, it was a celebration, not of victory *actually* won, but only of victory *promised*. The edict that secured the Jews' salvation was *announced*. But it was not yet *executed*. Nevertheless, there *was* joy. The promise, they knew, made the victory certain.

A More Sure Glory
The deliverance that has been promised to us as Christians, the victory that is ours in Jesus, is *more sure still*, our destiny certain, our future secure. Those whom God predestined He called, and whom He called He justified, and whom He justified, He glorified (Rom. 8:30). Note that last past tense. Those whom He called and justified He *glorified* – past tense. The glory to come, for a believer in the Lord Jesus Christ, is so sure that Paul speaks about it as though it were *already done*. One day all creation will be swept up into the glorious liberty of the children of God. And sin and death and sorrow and suffering will be undone forever.

Future Glory and Present Joy
Now if the Jews of Persia could rejoice at an earthly promise of political and military victory, where is *our* joy at the sure and certain hope of the resurrection to eternal life that is ours, sealed by *Christ's* blood – not a tyrant's signet ring – and guaranteed by His empty tomb? Does your Christian life reflect a deep awareness of the glory to follow, so sure and certain, kept in heaven for you, such that you cannot help but thrill at the goodness and grace of God, and rejoice in His promises? *You can measure your embrace of the promise of future glory by the practice of present joy.*

At the end of Tolkien's book, *The Lord of The Rings*, Sam, one of the central characters, awakens to find friends whom he thought dead, alive and all around him. 'Gandalf.' he said, 'I thought you were dead. But then I thought I was dead myself. *Is everything sad going to come untrue?* What's happened to the world?'

'"A great Shadow has departed," said Gandalf, and then he laughed and the sound was like music, or like water in a parched land.'[4] Fellow Christians, everything sad *is* going to come untrue. Christ is risen. A great *eucatastrophe* has occurred. Death is undone. A great Shadow has departed. Sin and death and hell have been defeated. The Lamb wins.

So let me ask you, where is your joy? *You can measure your embrace of the promise of future glory by the practice of present joy.*

A reward – let us not grow weary in doing good, for we shall reap if we do not give up.

A request – if Esther's importunity was answered by a tyrant king, how much more will ours be by our Father in heaven who loves to give good gifts to those who ask Him?

A reversal – the greatest *eucatastrophe* of them all is the empty tomb and the victory of the Resurrection, and one day, if we are Christians, we shall share in it all.

A rejoicing – everything sad *is* going to come untrue, therefore, let us praise the Lord.

---

4. J. R. R. Tolkien, *The Lord of The Rings*, *Vol. 3, Book 5: The Return of the King*, (London, UK: Harper Collins, 1991) 988.

9

Holy War
(Esther 9–10)

We come now to the conclusion of the Book of Esther. If you recall, wicked Haman's 'final solution' was to be the holocaust of the Jewish people. But, as we'll see, what happened was the climactic reversal in a book of sudden reversals. The Jews were delivered, and their enemies were destroyed, giving rise to the annual festival of Purim, celebrated by the Jewish people even to this day. For many of us, however, the details of Esther 9 and 10 are unsettling. They record terrible conflict and loss of life. They depict the public shaming of the bodies of Haman's sons. And they tell us that it is this blood-thirsty *dénouement* to the story of Esther that provides the rationale for an annual festival of celebration among the people of God. At a superficial level at least, Esther 9–10 takes what has been a wonderful tale, full of irony and biting wit as we are made to laugh out loud at the folly of the enemies of righteousness and the wisdom of God in saving His children from the worst jams imaginable – at a superficial level Esther 9 and 10 takes all that *and spoils it*. Instead of the joyous hilarity of surprising deliverance, the climactic notes of the book are dark indeed: full of the bitterness of judgment. We can't help but feel the sting of moral ambiguity when the good guys turn on the bad guys only to act like the bad guys themselves.

And we must immediately admit, before we get into the details of the story, the plausibility of those instincts. Let's be honest enough to confess that even the most godly are flawed, and that those flaws often reveal themselves most obviously when we find ourselves – like Esther and Mordecai do now – in a position of power and dominance. Aren't we often contrite and dependent on the Lord when we are weak, vulnerable, in trouble, only to become as mean as spit when we think we have the upper hand? So it's at least possible that something of that order is going on here. Now that the Lord has brought Mordecai and Esther from disenfranchised depths to sit in the heights of supreme power and privilege, they become mirror images of the tyrants they have displaced. Like the pigs in Orwell's *Animal Farm*, who, having displaced the farmer and his family, declare, 'All animals are equal, but some are more equal than others.' And as they begin to abuse their power their faces start to change to look just like the humans they overthrew. It happens all the time. As Lord Acton famously put it, 'Power tends to corrupt, and absolute power corrupts absolutely. *Great men are almost always bad men.*'[1] Could *that* be what is happening in Esther 9 and 10? Have Esther and Mordecai become tyrants in their own right? Has absolute power corrupted absolutely? Well, it's plausible… but I don't think so.

1. The Pattern of Sacred Conflict (9:1-19)

Esther has secured for herself and Mordecai the right to enact a new law, contradicting Haman's law to destroy the Jews. You can find the language of the new law in 8:11, 'the king allowed the Jews who were in every city to gather and defend their lives, to destroy, to kill and to annihilate any armed force of any people or province that might attack them, children and women included, and to plunder their goods.'

Chapter 9 opens as that day dawns, and we are immediately told what happens when the king's command and edict were about to be carried out, on the very day when the enemies of the Jews hoped to gain mastery over them, the reverse occurred: the Jews gained mastery over those who hated them. Helped by government officials, the Jews throughout

---

1. John E. E. Dalberg, Lord Acton, *Letter to Bishop Mandell Creighton, April 5, 1887*, published in *Historical Essays and Studies*, J. N. Figgis and R. V. Laurence eds. (London: Macmillan, 1907) 504.

the empire turn the tables on Haman's cut-throat mob. In verse 6 we're told that 500 men were killed in the capital. In verse 16 we're told that 75,000 were killed across the rest of the Persian Empire. And between these two statements, in verses 11-15, we have another interview between Ahasueras and Esther.

Ahasueras has heard reports of the battle on the streets of Susa. And, like the aristocratic sociopath he's shown himself to be, he's far from distressed at the carnage among his citizenry. In fact, he's quite impressed. 'Five-hundred slain in Susa, you say? Jolly good show. Let's see what they can do elsewhere.' And, almost by way of reward it seems, all unsolicited this time, he invites another unconditional, unlimited request from Esther, 'What is your wish? It shall be granted you. And what further is your request? It shall be fulfilled?' For some commentators what Esther says next is her darkest hour. She asks that the bloodshed in Susa be extended for another day, so that it might be taken out of the citadel down into the outer city, and so that the bodies of the ten sons of Haman might be publicly exposed to humiliation by being hung on their own gallows alongside their father. And we're left to think, 'She wants *more* blood?' And what do we make of the macabre business with Haman's sons?

Well, for that we need to come to terms with the scriptural tradition of holy war. We know that is what is going on here because of the three times in the text (v. 10, v. 15, v. 16) when our author makes a point of telling us that, amidst all the conflict and bloodshed, the Jews 'laid no hand on the plunder'. Mordecai's decree had expressly permitted them to do so, in keeping with the normal practice of Persian war. So, why didn't they plunder their enemies? The Jews didn't touch the plunder because they understood that the conflict in which they were engaged was not *political* merely, but *sacred* in nature. This is *holy war*.

Holy War in the Old Testament

In Genesis 14 Abram went to war to rescue his nephew, Lot, and when he came home triumphant the king of Sodom offered him the plunder. But Abram refused, lest *wicked Sodom* be said to be the source of his prosperity (Gen. 14:21-23). And from then onwards, especially during Israel's conquest of the Promised Land, they would touch nothing of the possessions of their enemies. So, after the defeat of Jericho, under Joshua's leadership, for example, Israel attacked the city of Ai only to be utterly defeated. The reason? Achan had stolen some of the plunder from Jericho for himself, and so Israel fell under divine displeasure. It was only when Achan himself was destroyed that their victory could be restored and Ai defeated (Josh. 7:1–8:29). Holy war required that Israel become the executor of divine judgment on the idolatry and immorality of the peoples into whose land they had come, and they were to destroy them utterly for their sin, *but to profit in no way from their wickedness.*

Now, you may recall that the backstory to the book of Esther is in fact a narrative of *failed holy war*. It is the history of King Saul, Israel's first king, and his war with the Amalekites, led by King Agag. Saul, like Achan before him, had failed to execute the principles of holy war. He left Agag alive, and plundered the best of the enemy's possessions, so that the prophet Samuel confronted him in these words, 'The Lord sent you on a mission, saying, "Go and completely destroy those wicked people, the Amalekites; make war on them until you have wiped them out." Why did you not obey the Lord? *Why did you pounce on the plunder and do evil in the eyes of the Lord?'* (1 Sam. 15:18-19).

And so, because of his failure to obey and execute holy war on Agag and the Amalekites, Saul was disqualified as Israel's king. And *now* in Esther 9, we meet Saul's descendants, Esther and Mordecai, leading God's people *as they rewrite their history of failure with one of new obedience.* They have unfinished business with the Amalekites. So they prosecute a new holy war, this time against Haman, the Agagite, the descendant of King Agag. So, when Esther asks for a second day to chase down those who sided with Haman the Agagite in the lower city of Susa, she is not asking out of blood lust and venom. *She is asking for permission to do what Saul never did. She wants to complete the task of holy war* – to 'make war on them until you have wiped them out'. Even the gruesome act of publicly displaying the bodies of Haman's sons was part of the tradition of ancient warfare: it is in fact the fate of Esther's ancestor King Saul and his sons. They were humiliated in this way on the walls of the Philistines in 1 Samuel 31:1-13. But now the tables have turned. A great reversal has occurred. It is the enemies put to open shame.

So, as brutal is it all no doubt was, we do need to understand that in conducting holy war, the people of God were engaged in something wholly other than a modern program of ethnic cleansing or geopolitical land grabbing. *They were prosecuting the decree of God in judgment upon His enemies.* It was, in fact, a graphic expression of a deeper conflict that has raged, really, since Genesis 3:15, when God declared that the Seed of the Woman and the seed of the Serpent would live in perpetual enmity till One would come who would crush the serpent's head.

Holy War at Calvary

Cain vs. Abel, Jacob vs. Esau, Isaac vs. Ishmael, Israel vs. the Amalekites, Saul vs. King Agag, and now Esther, Mordecai and the exiled Jews vs. Haman and his allies: all give expression to that age-old warfare which meets its final expression in the Lord Jesus Christ who prosecutes the climactic 'holy war' against Satan himself. Paul says in Colossians 2:15 that Jesus 'disarmed the rulers and authorities' – the satanic powers – 'and has put them to open shame', much like Haman and his sons were in our story. Here is *Christ's* holy war. But what is unique about *His* conquest, Paul says, is that *Jesus* triumphs over His enemies *in the cross*. The defeat of the devil and his allies, both supernatural and human, is achieved at Calvary, where, neither Satan, nor sinners, *but Christ* Himself was made to share Haman's cursed fate and was hung upon a tree.

Holy War in the Christian Life

Paul tells us as Christians that *we are still* locked in a deadly spiritual battle. The pattern of sacred conflict *continues*, though now 'We wrestle not against flesh and blood, but against the rulers, against the authorities, against the cosmic powers over this present darkness, against the spiritual forces of evil in the heavenly places' (Eph. 6:12). *That is the Christian life.* But as we see that, does it not help to remember that *our* conflict, unlike Esther's, is not waged against the backdrop of our king's past failures? No, *we* fight *in light of a Better King's perfect victory*. We are fighting a battle day by day with sin and the flesh and the devil. We're in conflict with worldviews that reject and deny the truth claims of the Christian gospel. We struggle constantly with the flesh and our own remaining corruption. *But we do not do so in any doubt about the final outcome*, for *we* know what *Esther* did not know. *We* know that the victory has already been won. Christ has 'disarmed the enemy, putting them to public shame, triumphing over them in the cross' (Col. 2:15). Which is why Paul can quote Genesis 3:15, the first promise of a Messiah who would crush Satan's head, and apply it, not to Jesus, but to us in Romans 16:20: 'the God of peace will soon crush Satan under *your* feet.' He will bring *us* into the very same victory *Jesus has already won*. He will crush Satan under *our* feet, because the Seed of the Woman has *already* crushed the serpent's head. Isn't that good news?

Some of you have become discouraged in your conflict with sin. You feel you will never overcome that besetting vice that seems to hold you ensnared. Your conscience sears and stings and you live with daily shame, longing for deliverance. 'Who can save me from this body of death?' (Rom. 7:24), you cry. Some of you are in contexts – an office, a hospital, a lecture theatre, even a home – where the claims of the gospel are constantly held up to ridicule and you are weary and bruised and wonder if you can go on. Cling to Romans 16:20. Remember that the holy war has *been* waged *and won* at the Cross, and that the promise of Genesis 3:15 is one you can plead for yourself, because it has already been kept *on your behalf in Christ*, 'the God of peace will crush Satan beneath *your* feet,' *because He has already done so at the Cross*. Do *not* give up. Fight on. Love on. Pray on. Keep on keeping on, in the knowledge that sin and Satan, cynicism and unbelief, will not win, because Jesus has already won.

2. The Principles of Spiritual Celebration (9:20-28)

Here are *the principles of spiritual celebration*. Mordecai records all these events in a letter mandating that the day of victory be observed as a holiday among the Jews, in perpetuity. They named the day Purim, after the *pur*, the lots, that Haman had cast to determine how and when to strike at the Jewish people. This was the day, selected by lot, intended by Haman for disaster, but which God intended for deliverance.

An Old Covenant Day of Joy and Gladness
And in the celebration of Purim the Jews were doing two things. *First*, they were *remembering*. They were remembering the remarkable providence of God, and His saving intervention, and the gift He gave them of relief from their enemies, as verse 22 puts it. That word *relief*, by the way, is really the word *rest*, which rings throughout scripture, but especially throughout Joshua and Judges – the books that are full of holy war – with connotations of God's saving blessing and mercy. They remember the saving rest God gave them from their enemies.

And the *second* thing they do as they remember the saving rest of grace is they *rejoice*: '…the month that had been turned for them from sorrow into gladness and from mourning into a holiday; that they should make them days of feasting and gladness, days for sending gifts of food to one another and gifts to the poor' (Esther 9:22). *The day that commemorated their victory became the perennial day of rejoicing and celebration.* The plot that intended to destroy them became the festival that would unite and sustain them amidst all the long years of trial and conflict ahead.

A New Covenant Day of Joy and Gladness
In many ways the application, the big idea, the answer to the question, 'What is the book of Esther *for*?' lies right here. According to Esther 9:20-28 this whole story is told to explain the festival of Purim. Esther is about remembering the saving rest of God's grace and rejoicing in it. That is what they were to do at Purim. And it is what Christians do every Lord's Day. On the first day of the week, when death was undone, and the stone rolled away, and life and immortality were brought to light in the resurrection of Jesus Christ (2 Tim. 1:10), we gather to remember the Sabbath rest of God, and to rejoice. Sunday is *our* festival day. The Christian Sabbath is our day for feasting and gladness, for giving and celebration. And a part of our task, as we seek to remember the Sabbath day to keep it holy (Exod. 20:8), is to rehearse again the victory of Jesus Christ, to tell and be told 'the old, old story of Jesus and

his Love'.[2] It is to remember the redemptive rest of God won at Calvary, so that, whatever the dark clouds of Monday to Saturday, on *this* day, the day when light was spoken into the darkness, and the light of the world rose in triumph, on *this* day, the light of the gospel might shine afresh into our darkness and the darkness never overcome it, that on *this* day our sorrow might be turned to gladness and our mourning into a holiday. If you think Sabbath observance is a *killjoy*, you've never understood nor kept the Sabbath rightly. It is a 'day of rest and gladness, a day of joy and light' on which to remember the redemptive rest won by Christ and rejoice.

3. The Priority of a Superior King (9:28–10:3)

The Book of Esther ends, quite wonderfully, by turning our gaze *away* from the duty of the people to remember and to celebrate Purim, and fixing our attention one last time on the principal actors in the drama. In 9:28-32 we focus on Queen Esther. She confirms Mordecai's decree. Here she is now, at last, come into her full royal and legislative authority, acting like the queen she has grown to become. And then in 10:1-3 we focus on Mordecai: his high honor and privilege and his great popularity among the Jews because he 'sought the welfare of his people and spoke peace to all his people.'

Esther and Mordecai take on almost Messianic status here. The last sights the author wants to fill our gaze with are visions of these two, who have been the instruments of God's redemption of His people. *But He can't quite do it.* There is one discordant note in his otherwise harmonious final song. Look at 10:1: 'Ahasueras imposed tax on the land and on the coastlands of the sea. And all the acts of *his* power and might...are written in the book of the Chronicles of the kings of Media and Persia.' *Even when talking about Mordecai, he is still only 'second in rank to King Ahasueras'*, great among the Jews perhaps, *but still not king.*

Fixing our Eyes on a Better King
For all Esther's political power and all Mordecai's personal popularity, they remained subjects of tyrannical, sociopathic,

---

2. Refrain from the hymn lyrics 'I Love to Tell the Story' by A. Katherine Hankey.

volatile, amoral Ahasueras. *He* is the one still on the throne. We get to the end of Esther, with its stunning victory and the jubilation of the people of God, and the author very carefully and very deliberately drops a fly into the honey. 'Don't get carried away. The final victory isn't here yet,' he's saying. 'The true savior has not come yet. A *Better King* is what we need. Look *there*, not at Esther, not at Mordecai.'

And so, as we take our leave of this book *that*, surely, is the most helpful thing it can teach us. It is, in the end, a call to look to Jesus, 'the founder and perfecter of our faith, who, for the joy that was set before him, endured the cross, despising the shame, and is seated at the right hand of the throne of God' (Heb. 12:2). We are to 'see Jesus, who for a little while was made lower than the angels, now crowned with glory and honor because of the suffering of death, so that by the grace of God he might taste death for everyone' (Heb. 2:9). No mere man or woman will do. Dear reader, do not put your trust, nor seek your comfort, nor locate your value, in the ministry of your pastors, or in the love of your spouses, or in the successes of your children, much less in yourselves. Look to Christ. We need a Better King, the true and only Savior. So fix your eyes upon *Him*.

Bibliography

Dalberg, John E. E., Lord Acton, *Historical Essays and Studies*, J. N. Figgis and R. V. Laurence eds. (London: Macmillan, 1907).

Duguid, Iain, *Esther and Ruth* (Phillipsburg, NJ: P&R Publishing, 2005).

Firth, David G., *The Message of Esther* (Downers Grove, IL: InterVarsity Press 2010).

Henry, Matthew, *Commentary on the Whole Bible, Vol. II.* (New York: Revell, 1983).

Jobes, Karen H., *Esther, NIVAPC* (Grand Rapids, MI: Zondervan 1999).

Tolkien, J. R. R., *The Letters of J. R. R. Tolkien* (London: Harper Collins, 2012), Letter 89.

Westminster Shorter Catechism, The, www.si.com/vault/2009/03/16/105787321/ the-shot-that-saved-lives.

Subject Index

Scripture Index

Other books in the Focus on the Bible commentary series

Other books in the Focus on the Bible commentary series

Christian Focus Publications

Our mission statement –

STAYING FAITHFUL
In dependence upon God we seek to impact the world through literature faithful to His infallible Word, the Bible. Our aim is to ensure that the Lord Jesus Christ is presented as the only hope to obtain forgiveness of sin, live a useful life and look forward to heaven with Him.

Our books are published in four imprints:

CHRISTIAN
FOCUS

Popular works including biographies, commentaries, basic doctrine and Christian living.

CHRISTIAN
HERITAGE

Books representing some of the best material from the rich heritage of the church.

MENTOR

Books written at a level suitable for Bible College and seminary students, pastors, and other serious readers. The imprint includes commentaries, doctrinal studies, examination of current issues and church history.

CF4•K

Children's books for quality Bible teaching and for all age groups: Sunday school curriculum, puzzle and activity books; personal and family devotional titles, biographies and inspirational stories – because you are never too young to know Jesus!

Christian Focus Publications Ltd,
Geanies House, Fearn, Ross-shire,
IV20 1TW, Scotland, United Kingdom.
www.christianfocus.com